JESUS SAID TO HER

Life's Secrets from Conversations with Women

Skip Moen

Copyright 2010

Scripture quotations taken from the New American Standard Bible®, Copyright © 1960, 1962, 1963, 1968, 1971, 1972, 1973, 1975, 1977, 1995 by The Lockman Foundation Used by permission." (www.Lockman.org)

INTRODUCTION

Women's studies have become a focal point of the modern world. For more than a generation, the role of women has grown significantly in every part of life. This change is long overdue, especially within Christian circles. It is now a cliché to say that Jesus revolutionized the world's perspective on women, although it took men nearly two millennia to recognize what He did. It would be foolish for me, a twenty-first century male, to even begin to comment on the ground usefully uncovered by many skillful and intelligent women. But perhaps there is something I can add – a look at the timeless truths that fell from the lips of Jesus in his encounters with the women of his world.

This collection is not meant for women alone. God is no respecter of gender. Although Jesus[1] provided us with pictures of the nature of God through His brief dialogues with women, these pictures speak to everyone. Yeshua simply chose these women to show us something deep and important about all of us.

In these glimpses, we will focus on just a few panes of much bigger windows into Yeshua's interaction with women. These are not intended to give you the entire story. They are samplers, enough to interest the taste buds but not sate the appetite. Behind these short and succinct studies lies a much bigger work – a work that stands on the shoulders of many scholars and cultural pioneers. If you find in the words of the Master Teacher what I

---

[1] I believe it is important to learn and use the real Hebrew name of our Lord. That name is not "Jesus." It is Yeshua. There is a long linguistic story behind this change, but now that we know, we should begin using it. So in this book, you will find our Savior referred to as Yeshua. He's the same person, but at least now we can call him by the name he was given in Hebrew.

find, you will soon hunger for more. The Feast of the Lamb promises to be overwhelmingly better.

Skip Moen

TABLE OF CONTENTS

Expectation: What Do You Want? A Look At John 2:4	1
Exclusion: Why Don't I Belong? A Look At Matthew 9:20	11
Hopelessness: Who Really Cares About Me? A Look At Luke 13:12	25
Rejection: Do You See Me? A Look At Matthew 15:28	37
Remorse: Can I Forgive Myself? A Look At Luke 7:50	54
Loss: How Can I Go On? A Look At John 12:7	67
Thanklessness: Does Anyone Treasure Me? A Look At Luke 10:42	75
Grief: Who Will Care For Me Now? A Look At Luke 7:13	90
Mission: What Should I Do? A Look At Matthew 28:10	101
Fulfillment: Is There More Than This? A Look At Matthew 20:21	112

Connection: Won't Someone Help Me? A Look At Mark 5:41	117
Worry: What If Something Terrible Happens? A Look At Luke 2:49	128
Blessing: Why Can't I Be The Lucky One? A Look At Luke 11:28	136
Destiny: What Was I Made For? A Look At Luke 23:28	143
Insight: How Can This Be? A Look At John 11:26	151
Remembering: How Could I Forget? A Look At John 11:39	162
Equality: Why Do You Think I'm Different? A Look At John 4:26	166
Submission: Why Should I Serve You? A Look At Genesis 16:8	182
Yeshua and Women	193

EXPECTATION

What do you want?

Wouldn't it be nice if everything went according to plan? Just think of the relief we would experience if we knew that nothing unexpected would pop up during the day. But life rarely cooperates with our need for organized self-sufficiency. We have to deal with interruptions. It doesn't seem to matter if we are busy executives or unhurried contemplatives. Life goes its own way and we must adapt.

There is a great lesson to be learned in this ordered chaos. God greets us in interruptions and unexpected situations. He designed life to provide these openings where we are forced to look for Him. He loves these slices of human confusion because they push us to recognize our deeper dependence. It was no different in the days when Yeshua walked in Palestine. Dealing with unexpected situations forces us to reflect on our egocentric need for control and on God's magnificent surprises.

The story in John 2:1-11

"Woman, what do I have to do with you?" John 2:4

Have you noticed how much time women spend trying to keep the peace between people? Perhaps it is the built-in result of being mothers. Maybe it's just genetic. But it seems that when conflict arises, women do their best to act as peacemakers.

Men, on the other hand, seem to be much more hardheaded. They have the flight or fight syndrome. Just get out or else prepare for battle. I don't think this is a result of left over Neanderthal aggression. A lot of this difference comes from childhood training processes. Most boys learn about life through games of competition. They are taught values through defeating others. But girls learn games of cooperation. Their early childhood play is inclusive. They may compete, but their competition is much more subtle. That training has a lot to do with their worldview.[2]

In this story, Yeshua's mother is trying to keep the peace. The first miracle in the gospel of John is about social expectations. After Yeshua gathers a few of the disciples, he attends a wedding. Mary is also one of the guests. It becomes obvious to her that the wedding party will soon run out of wine. She wants to rescue the situation and prevent a conflict. So, she decides to take the issue to her oldest son.

We are apt to read our own cultural bias into this conversation between Yeshua and his mother. At first glance, Yeshua seems insensitive. He seems to be acting like a typical male. Why would Yeshua address his own mother with such a cold expression? The Greek word *gunai* commonly means woman or wife. The surprising element of this verse is not the translation but the tone. We are a gender sensitive culture, so this translation seems to depict Yeshua speaking harshly to his mother, questioning why she is bothering him about so insignificant a fact as no wine at a wedding. While the English wording is correct, we lose the real emotion in this translation.

In some respects, this verse seems like the one thing that every mother fears – rejection by one of her children. Mary is at the wedding. She is thrilled to have her oldest son there. She is proud,

---

[2] A very insightful woman, Deborah Tannen, noted all this in *You Just Don't Understand* (Quill, 2001).

perhaps much more so than anyone can realize. The absence of her husband Joseph probably indicates that he has died. So, Yeshua is the "man of the house" now. She relies on him. She knows that he can take care of things. When she realizes that there is a social embarrassment in the making, she goes to her reliable refuge – Yeshua, the good son. But it looks as though Yeshua says something that would unnerve any mother's expectations.

"Mother, please! What does bad wedding planning have to do with me?", as if to imply that this kind of problem is not really a problem that should be brought to the attention of the God-Man. If we read the verse like this, we will be greatly mistaken – and we will miss a very important lesson. In order to understand the real emotions here, we need to look at other uses of this word translated "woman."

Yeshua uses this same Greek word in moments of great tenderness, for example, when he transfers earthly responsibility for care of his mother to John as he is dying on the cross and when he speaks to Mary Magdalene at the tomb. It is not a cold and sterile rejection. Our modern translations remove the tone of voice. We are inclined to think that Yeshua is separating himself from the concerns of his mother. That is a mistake. Yeshua is actually being tender.

But it is not just the tone that is missing. The way that Yeshua frames his response to Mary has been altered. It might not be good English grammar, but the chopped-up word order in the Greek text tells us something we need to know. This verse literally says:

"What to me and to you, woman?"

Do you see that Yeshua is not isolating himself from Mary at all? He includes both of them in the situation. His expression is "to me and to you." Yeshua makes both of them a part of this problem, and part of the question about its solution. Yeshua is not saying, "Why are *you* bothering *me*?" He is saying, "How are *we* related to this issue?" Yeshua is inviting her into the solution. He seeks her cooperation.

Yeshua is not playing the stern male. He is not correcting her or belittling her. He acknowledges her concern with tenderness. He asks Mary how this matter connects *them*. Yeshua does not cast her aside. He invites her to join him in the solution. With tenderness, he salutes her role in his life – and then he asks if she understands his role in her life. What does this thing have to do with *us*? How will this issue bring us together?

No problem is too small to put before Yeshua – not even wine at a wedding. But do not be surprised if the problem raises a different question – a question that includes you in the solution, a question that asks about your relationship to him *before* both of you decide what to do.

Yeshua puts the same question before each of us. We come to him with some problem. It may not even be *our* problem. We may, like Mary, be looking for a solution for someone else. But when we place the problem before Yeshua, he does not ask, "What do you want me to do?" He asks, "How does this thing bring us together?" The lesson is simple: the problem we see is only a window that opens a relationship with Him. It's not about the wine. It's about the willingness to enter into the problem together.

Mary came to Yeshua because she expected Yeshua to provide a solution. She did not anticipate the surprising question: "How does this problem bring us into fellowship with each other?" She thought she could leave the matter with him. He asked her to re-examine the roles and validate the relationship. The unanticipated event became an opening for something much more important. God showed up in a simple question.

Expectation. Interruption. Surprise. Re-orientation. Are you watching for God in all the wrong places?

Expectation (2)

"Woman, what do I have to do with you?" John 2:4

People with problems often confronted Yeshua. The blind man, the lepers, the father with a sick child, the woman with a hemorrhage – they all came to him hoping for relief. In every case, he showed compassion. In fact, on more than one occasion he corrected the thinking of the disciples by pointing out that what appeared to be tragedy in life was simply the opportunity for God's glory to be displayed.

Our spiritual sensitivity agrees. We picture those poor, diseased bodies in need of God's healing touch. We expect Yeshua to respond. After all, he said that his mission was to give sight to the blind, heal the sick and preach the gospel to the poor. But wine at a wedding? It just doesn't seem to fall into the same category. It's not "religious" enough to qualify as an opportunity for God to intervene. Nevertheless, we see Yeshua respond tenderly to Mary, including her in this issue.

But the next question indicates that there has been a change in Yeshua's relationship with his mother. He is deliberately stepping away from those old family associations. He is beginning a new chapter in his life, a chapter that will take him to the cross. Now only the Father directs his life. Even though there is tenderness, nothing will distract him from doing the Father's will. "My hour has not yet come" is Yeshua's point of separation from all humanity, even his own mother. For thirty years he has been responsive to her concerns. Now things are changing.

"What (does this mean) to me and what (do you think it means) to you, special woman?"

This is not a rhetorical question. Yeshua is asking Mary to think deeply about the relationship change. He does not dismiss her or her concern. He only shows her that something else has now taken center stage.

Be Mary for a moment. You know that this son, the one you brought into the world through your own body, is a very special man. Not like a single other man ever before. You know that God Himself is the reason for this man's existence. For thirty years you have watched him grow. He nursed at your breast. He slept in your arms. You taught him to walk, to speak and to become a child of God. And you watched him become the man of God's choosing. Now he has assumed the role that you knew he was destined to achieve. People are beginning to follow him, as you knew they would. His reputation is growing. You feel the pride and the confirmation, after all those years of patiently waiting. There is nothing he can't do. You know this more than any other mother in history. This small problem about wine is insignificant compared to the things you hope for your son, the one who will free his people. So, it seems natural to bring this issue to Yeshua. What mother wouldn't?

Most of our relationships with other people require accommodations. God knows all about that fact, and He gives us plenty of useful information about how we are to conduct those relationships. Husbands, love your wives. Wives, choose to obey your husbands. Children, honor your parents. Young men, respect your elders. Lots of accommodations. But there is one relationship that must never be compromised, even if intimate family members are in the mix. "Love God with all your heart, mind and strength" does not give room for diverting attention to someone else. God always comes first.

In this verse, Yeshua draws a line. He acknowledges with tenderness that it is a special woman who asks him to act. But he is no longer under her authority. He serves the Father only. This first miracle in the Gospel of John is a dividing line between the Yeshua who grew up in the family of Joseph and Mary and the Yeshua who becomes the hoped-for Messiah with a new family of God's elect.

Nevertheless, Yeshua still turns the water into wine. He draws the line and then he draws a circle. The line says, "I have been born for one special purpose." The circle says, "Every circumstance in life is an intersection with the divine." The line says, "There is only one master that I serve." The circle says, "Honoring my father and mother is service to Him." Old relationships must change if we are to separate ourselves to God's purposes. Tenderness must meet commitment. But one does not exclude the other.

When we model Yeshua's action, we draw a line on the ground. It says, "I live in the service of my Lord. Nothing will come between His wishes and my actions." But then we draw a circle. The circle says, "How may I serve you in the name of my Lord." In this lesson we learn that commitment meets service in the act of love.

Expectation (3)

"Woman, what do I have to do with you?" John 2:4

"Whatever he says to you, do it" John 2:5

Mary got it. She understood the change in her relationship with Yeshua. Her reaction is incredibly important in this story. She deliberately shifts the authority to him. She stopped expecting. She left the rest of the story entirely up to him.

The words "do it" are the Greek word *poiesate*. It is from the verb *poieo* that means "to make, to do, to cause, to bring about, to produce." Mary is telling everyone to follow the directions of her son without regard to their personal evaluation. It is a command. In Greek, the word "it" is implied. What Mary really says is "Whatever he says, **do!**"

Often mothers give the best advice. Mary knew what she was talking about. If Yeshua tells you to do something, just do it. Don't hesitate. Don't debate. Don't start an internal process of questioning why or how or when. Mary is the original Nike commercial. **Just do it!**

Mary understood something that we often seem to miss. She knew the character of her son. She knew that he always did what was right. So, there was never any need to second-guess his motives or his directions. She knew that following his orders would always result in just the right thing.

Did you notice that Mary is directing those who really did not know him to follow his orders? Why would they do that? Because they were the household servants and they were used to following the orders of one in authority. And did you notice that Mary does not say, "Follow *my* orders." She tells them to listen to Yeshua.

Mary came to Yeshua expecting him to meet a need. Yeshua asked her to let go of those expectations. She did. Do you see that she releases all of her concerns to his control? She no longer tries to manage the rescue operation. She turns it all over to him.

What Mary told those servants long ago is something we need to listen to today. We are still the household servants under God's rule. We need the attitude "whatever he says, I do." He is my commander-in-chief. There is no room for questioning or debating. There is only room for obedience. Become a first century shoe commercial for Christ – **Just do it!**

Now that we see both sides of this conversation, we need to remember one more point. This problem was not "too small" for Yeshua. It was not irreligious or unspiritual. Just like all of the other circumstances of life, it was one more opportunity to display God's glory. It was God's purpose hidden in a water pot.

If you read the rest of this little story, you know that the wedding party never knew this miracle occurred. Only the servants saw it happen. This is also important. The ones who were privileged to see God's glory in a water pot were the ones who obeyed the commands of His Son. Everyone else missed it.

It is worth pointing out that Yeshua did more than provide the finest drink at the feast. Under Jewish custom, the family of the groom could face legal penalties for failure to provide adequately at a wedding. Yeshua rescued this newly formed marriage from financial disaster. In addition, Yeshua gave them a substantial economic gift. If each water pot held 20 gallons and all six water pots became wine, this miracle provide the couple with something that could be sold for gain. It's unlikely that the wedding party would drink all of it on that day.

Water turned to wine. This odd miracle at the beginning of Yeshua' ministry shows us some important lessons:

Not a single circumstance of life is outside the scope of God's revealed glory. Everything is an opportunity to see His handiwork and praise Him.

Yeshua is both with us and apart from us. Life with Him is both a line and a circle.

Yeshua always *includes* us. His questions to us ask if we are willing to cooperate with him.

Our cooperation means letting go of our expectations.

What woman has more right to expectations than a mother? But Yeshua teaches us a different perspective about expectations. Yeshua drew Mary into the circle with him and then tenderly asked her to let go of her expectations. Yeshua teaches us that expectations must give way to trust. The solution to the problem is really about dependence. Whatever he says, do!

EXCLUSION

Why Don't I Belong?

Our world is a world of cliques. There are the "in" people and the "outsiders," the beautiful and the ignored, the rich and famous and all the rest of us. If we are to believe the obsession of the pundits, most of us will be forever disappointed with life. As the saying goes, "You can never be too rich or too thin." Our hypocritical world practices exclusion while it preaches tolerance. But just try to break into one of those cliques and you will soon discover that tolerance is merely a politically correct term devoid of any real embrace. Every woman knows what it means to be on the outside. It hurts. Maybe that's why we all try to draw the circle around us so that we can say, "Look at me. I count. I'm on the inside." From the church to the office, we are sociologically discriminating. Not everyone gets in. Not everyone meets the criteria. If we are going to be on the inside, someone must be on the outside.

Yeshua once encountered a woman who had been excluded for more than a decade. She was the victim of social intolerance, carefully concealed under the banner of religious law. It did not matter what she believed. She was not wanted. She was defiled. She was contagious. Her struggle and her faith to reach beyond the social protocol shows us something about the heart of God – and the value of God's interruptions.

The story in Matthew 9:18-22

"Daughter, take courage; your faith has made you well." Matthew 9:20

How often have you heard the story of the woman who touched the fringe of Yeshua's robe? Probably so often that you no longer hear what the words say. It is so familiar that the deep meaning has been lost. This is not a story about illness. It is a story about isolation. It is a story about the loss of family, fellowship and community when something in your life drives others away. It is a story about desperation.

To capture the power of Yeshua's words to this sick woman, we must repaint the picture.

Yeshua was a healer. Everyone knew it. Many saw him cure the sick. His reputation spread like wildfire through a land that was desperate for heroes and healers. So the crowds followed and pressed, straining to see another wonder. On this day, Yeshua encountered an official from the synagogue. His daughter died. But this did not deter him. He makes a spectacular statement of faith for a man in his position. "Come and lay your hand on her and she will live."

No one had seen such a miracle. But they believed. After all, hadn't Elijah raised the son of the widow of Zarephath? And wasn't it possible that this man who they called Yeshua was really Elijah come back from heaven? An official of the synagogue would certainly know the story from Israel's history. And if anyone deserved to receive such a blessing from God, it certainly would be an innocent child. So he begged Yeshua, "Just come and put your hand on her."

Yeshua does not hesitate. The Greek tells us that he immediately took action. He followed the official on the way to his home. But as he was walking with the crowd, something happened.

In that crowd, hidden from scrutiny, was a woman with a problem. The Greek word is *haimorroousa*. This is the word that becomes *hemorrhage* in English. It literally means, "flow of blood." The cause of this flow is not important. What is important is that this problem created ritual impurity for this woman. Blood flows were part of specific religious legislation. Women were considered religiously unclean during menstruation. Moreover, anyone who touched them, any article of clothing or any object that came into contact with them was also considered unclean. While this condition was usually temporary, for this woman the problem had taken over her life. Since she had been hemorrhaging for twelve years, she was excluded from the pious community all that time. So were those who had close contact with her. Her hidden problem created a very public humiliation and excluded her from fellowship. She was outside the circle.

Imagine twelve years of excommunication for something that was no fault of yours. Imagine the emotional trauma of those years, knowing that you could not share human touch without passing this religious stigma on to the ones you loved. No tenderness with your children. No intimacy with your spouse. No fellowship with your friends. No admittance to worship. How do you find God in the midst of unceasing rejection? So, she devised a plan.

Had anyone in the crowd realized she was there, they would have avoided her. She literally had the plague – the plague of being unclean. But she saw her opportunity. The crowd was entirely focused on Yeshua and the synagogue official. No one was paying her any attention. And she knew that if Yeshua could raise the dead, he could certainly take away her impurity. As far as she was concerned, she had been dead for twelve years, alive in body but separated from everyone she cared for. She was the walking dead, a ghost in the group. Now she had a chance to come alive again.

She approached Yeshua from behind. Doesn't this seem strange to you? Yeshua is about to applaud her courage and yet she sneaks up from behind. That doesn't sound like courage. It is more descriptive of cowardice. We will discover that Yeshua has something else in mind when he calls her courageous.

Leviticus 17:27 suggests that whoever comes in contact with a defiled person is also defiled. The action she plans will defile the man who is on his way to revive an innocent child. Now she faces her first terror.

"If I touch him, will God withdraw from him? Will he be unable to raise the child? Will they know it is because of me? Will my need mean this child will stay dead?"

Every Rabbi would have answered, "Yes!" God can't work through defiled people. She faced an incredible moral dilemma. "Should I take this step to heal myself and risk the life of a child? Or should I continue to live as though I were dead, never knowing if I will be able to hold my own children again?" Courage! Absolutely. She risked defiling the very one she needed to cure her. She risked preventing the healing of the child of the synagogue official.

Desperate people do desperate things. This is a story of desperation. But it is not a story of rejection. The first step of reaching for Yeshua must come from *my personal sense of desperation*. As long as I stand back in the crowd and say to myself, "No wait, that person needs Yeshua more than I do," I will never be healed. That posture assumes I know what God can handle and what God will do. For that perspective, I end up telling God how His grace should be manifest. No, I must take a different approach. I must come to the absolute end of myself - ready to do whatever it takes to touch the Master. This act of desperation is my act of total surrender. In that moment, my excommunication from His grace will become a weight so heavy that I cannot live without His mercy. And in that moment, I will find something wonderful. God is for me! My need does not blot out His mercy for others. My sin and rejection does not prevent his grace. He can take my guilt away.

This woman's discovery is a lesson for all of us. God's mercy is big enough. It is big enough to cover all the needs. Take the risk! Put your rejection, your guilt, your shame and your *curse* on Him and discover that there is enough for you – and for me. He is able!

Exclusion (2)

"Daughter, take courage; your faith has made you well." Matthew 9:20

Often a single act of courage is enough. But sometimes one act summarizes years of hidden struggles. The woman who touches Yeshua' robe was a woman whose courage took many forms.

Matthew makes it quite clear that she touches the "fringe" of Yeshua robe. This is not the hem. It is a tassel fringe that was worn by those who were recognized as a Rabbi. It had special significance because it reminded the wearer of the sacred law (Numbers 15:38).

This woman was ready to risk more than making Yeshua "unclean". She was ready to risk God's wrath by touching the very symbol of the Law that made her unclean. God struck down a man who only tried to prevent the Ark of the Covenant from falling. Wouldn't God take vengeance on a woman who defiled His holy Law?

"Better to be dead than to be the living dead," she thought. So she reached toward Yeshua.

The verb used to describe her touch is *hápto*. Greek distinguishes more than one meaning to the idea of touch. This verb means, "to handle something with the intention of influencing it." There is another Greek verb that we translate "touch" but it means to gently contact, like playing a musical instrument. We sometimes think that because this woman came up behind Yeshua, she only brushed against his robe. But that is not the sense of this word. She took the tassel in her hand and held it, hoping that her grasping would influence the outcome. She wasn't tentative at all. She grabbed and held on.

We can easily understand why Yeshua knew someone touched him. He felt the tug on his robe. But Yeshua' awareness was not limited to the physical pressure. While Matthew does not mention it, Luke says that Yeshua immediately knew that power went out from him (Luke 8:46). Only two people in the crowd knew what had happened. All the others were oblivious to the touch of defilement.

Matthew tells us what she was thinking. It is this insight that makes all the difference in this story. The woman thinks, "If only I can grasp the tassel, I will be *cured*." But this is not the end of the story. Matthew uses the word *sozo*. It really means "saved" and it implies a great deal more than physical recovery. This word occurs 54 times in the gospels. In nearly every case, it means, "to rescue from death, to deliver, to save from danger." Now we see that she knew full well that she was as good as dead. She did not need medical attention. She needed a lifesaver. The irony is that Yeshua was on his way to save another life when he encountered a woman who was already dead. She thought, "If he can raise a child from the dead, he can deliver me from death too."

Her courage needed to overcome something else. It is this hidden obstacle that makes the story so important. *She needed the courage to overcome guilt*. Under the Rabbinic law, her condition was not an accident. Bad things only happened to people who deserved them. The presence of physical illness or deformity was interpreted as a clear sign of God's imminent judgment for sin. This woman was unclean not simply because she was hemorrhaging. She was unclean because according to her religion she was outside of God's favor. She needed incredible courage in order to act against this belief. But desperation often overcomes guilt and hesitation. This woman fulfilled the conditions of the first Beatitude. She was willing to do anything. She was a *beggar* for God.

How many times has the presence of some characteristic in our own lives given rise to this terrible thought? If I struggle with some illness or traumatic circumstance, am I not tempted to believe that this is God's way of punishing me? How many of us, in the face of life-changing traumas, have gone through the exercise of searching our past to find some sin that we have not confessed or some person we have accidentally wronged? This woman's story is *our story*. We are plagued with guilt. And just like her flow of blood, guilt separates us from the grace of God.

The woman's courage was not confined to breaking the religious rules. It reached to heaven and cried out, "God, even if I am guilty, have mercy on me!" For twelve years she lived under the law of punishment. Punishment for something beyond her control. Punishment for being alive. How many of us have lived just like her? Wondering every day why God's grace doesn't seem to deliver us. Wondering if the God of mercy isn't really the God of revenge.

Learn from twelve years of isolation. God has the power to deliver us from the curses we inherit. We too must have the courage to believe, not that God can heal but that God can deliver! We don't want a cure; we want salvation. We want to experience the God who delivers *me* from the uncleanness of my guilt!

- What are your hidden struggles?
- Do you believe that facing yourself + facing these hidden struggles face to face w/ Jesus will open / break the curse (bonding up) these struggles bring?
- It takes courage to overcome guilt — bad choices...
- Are you willing to do anything for God? To know God...

Exclusion (3)

"Daughter, take courage; your faith has made you well." Matthew 9:20

"Someone touched me; I know that power has gone out from me." Luke 8:46

Luke's account adds an amazing detail. Yeshua recognized immediately that power left him. Do you realize how extraordinary this statement really is? Have any of us every felt anything like this? We often imagine that this awareness was the result of Yeshua's divinity. But I wonder if we have not overlooked the claim Yeshua continuously made. He did nothing on his own but only through his relationship with the Father. Here God the Father operates through Yeshua without Yeshua's volitional awareness. Yeshua says, "Who was touching me?" Does theological presupposition override the plain meaning of this statement? Yeshua did not know who it was. He is not fabricating a small white lie for the purpose of exposing a greater glory. He is human too. He knew that God met someone's cry for help, but he did not know who it was. Don't be surprised that Yeshua utters a decidedly human question.

Luke tells us that the woman realized she was unhidden. How important it is to see the root of this expression. *Lanthano* means, "to conceal, to cover or be unknown." With heart pumping and body shaking, she realizes that her attempts at *lanthano* are undone. The Greek word for *truth* is constructed from this root. The choice of this Greek word helps us see that truth is uncovering what is hidden. This woman encountered God's grace and that encounter could not remain hidden. The truth of her faith was revealed.

So she came forward, trembling. Trembling is not nearly strong enough. The word means "dread, terrified with fear." Play the scene in your mind. Put your emotions into it. It happened so quickly she could not pull back. As soon as she grasped the tassel, he stopped and asked the question. She pulled back her hand with a sudden jerk, but it was too late. He knew. Adrenaline shot through her. She nearly fainted, staggering backward against the crowd. She sought to escape but it was impossible now. The crowd was mesmerized by Yeshua's question. She was weak, knowing that her sin had been discovered. She anticipated the worst. Condemnation. Castigation. She had dared to expect God to meet her need. And she was a "nothing," an outcast, one of the defiled. How could she have ever thought God was for her?

Have you ever found yourself revealed? There is that blinding flash of something more than guilt. It is shame. Guilt is about my standing before the law. Guilt is my legal condition. Guilty says that no matter what my motivation, I have violated a legal requirement. But shame is something else. Shame is about my very identity as a person. Guilt says my action was wrong. Shame says I am wrong. Shame says that who I am is worthless. Shame is about my very existence. I can still have personal self-worth and admit guilt. But shame robs me of my dignity. It tells me I am nothing.

The woman fell down before Yeshua. She was battling both guilt and shame. She acknowledged her "sin" of defilement, but now shame burst upon her. The unclean, the cast out, the one whom God was punishing, had dared to say, "I believe." The text says that she *declared* before everyone what she had done. She made her guilt and her shame known.

There are few among us who are able to do what this woman did. Perhaps we are not desperate enough. But when events divinely conspire to bring us to the place where we confess both guilt and shame, we are truly tortured souls. It is so much easier to tell it all to God in secret. But secrets have power over us, even when they are confessed to the Lord. To break the terrible power of a secret requires declaration. Every psychologist knows this truth. So does every mother. Confession is good for much more than the soul.

Something happened when this woman revealed her guilt and her shame. Yeshua turned and looked at her before he spoke. The crowd was moving in one direction. Yeshua turned in the opposite direction. The Greek verb tells us that he turned himself around. Imagine the effect this had on the woman. For twelve years she went unrecognized. For twelve years she was deliberately avoided. For twelve years people looked right through her. In a moment of utter desperation, she does something forbidden. And immediately she is in the spotlight. Yeshua turns his attention (and the attention of everyone else) completely on her. If she thought she would silently find God's grace, she was mistaken. Her act of desperation has suddenly come to center stage. She is unhidden. God's answer to her desperation cannot be concealed. It floods the story with light.

Looking directly at her, Yeshua says, "Take courage, daughter." Put yourself in the sandals of this woman. Do you see that Yeshua is not addressing her act of handling the tassel? That moment of desperate courage has already past. Yeshua is not commending what she has already done. He is speaking to her emotional state in the moment she is pushed into the spotlight. He is addressing her need for affirmation. God really is for you. God accepts your desperate act. Yeshua might as well have said, "Blessed are you, one of the poor in spirit[3], for this day the kingdom of heaven has arrived to answer your cry."

"Take courage" is an announcement that God accepts you. It is not a command to reach out and touch. It is a command to embrace God's approval. The verb is *tharseo*. In the New Testament, it is only found as an imperative – a command – and only as a word of encouragement. Rejoice! Have hope! Be confident! God accepts you. You have been delivered from guilt! Yeshua is telling this woman that all of her fears can be set aside. She has not defiled God's Law. She has not disturbed God's plans. She has not brought condemnation. Her decision has been the channel of God's grace. Not only is she a living example of the first Beatitude, she is a confirmation of the power of grace over legalism.

"Your faith has delivered you." Remember the Greek verb *sozo*. The woman thought to herself, "If I can only grasp the tassel, I will be delivered (*sozo*)." And this is exactly what Yeshua confirms. "Your faith has delivered (*sozo*) you." You have been rescued from death. You have been saved. Not just cured. Not just made whole. You have discovered something far deeper. You have discovered that God arrived to lift you above the guilt of the Law and the morass of shame. God has whispered in your ear, "You are of value to me."

Yeshua's use of *sozo* is in the perfect tense. In Greek, this indicates a completed action in the past that has continuing consequences for the present. Did you notice that Yeshua acknowledges that the deliverance is already accomplished? He did not say, "You are

---

[3] The Greek word is *ptochos*. It is not about the working poor. It is about those who are destitute, the beggars of society who will die unless they receive alms. These people cannot *afford* pride.

now made whole." He announces that her deliverance already occurred, and that it will continue. She is no longer dead. She has been brought back to life. It is not enough to say that she has been healed of the hemorrhage. She has been healed of the load of guilt she carried all those years. She has been reaffirmed as a valuable child of the Father. This act of faith encompasses her body, mind and soul. It removes the constraint of the Law and the weight of insignificance. In one impossible moment, God answered and grace permeated her life.

Yeshua blesses her. She is not only well, she is accepted. What she lost most in her defilement was community. What Yeshua gives her is fellowship. Her guilt is removed. God is not punishing her for some unknown sin. Her shame is cast away. She is reinstated in the kingdom of the delivered.

Yeshua final words to this woman are the words everyone who has known guilt and shame longs to hear: "Go in peace." These are words of eternal harmony between God and Man and between men. Peace (*shalom*) is the word that announces return to community. It *includes* me.

This story is about each of us. We carry the bloody mess of guilt as a sign of separation. Guilt destroys us. It segregates us from each other. It isolates us from God. It saps the life from us until we are nothing more than the walking dead. We go through the motions of living without the hope of redemption. If we live with guilt long enough, we inherit shame. We start to believe that we cannot be worthy. But one day we reach a point of desperation where we are willing to do anything to be delivered. We are ready to die if need be, but we refuse to just exist.

"Take courage," says Yeshua. Rejoice. God delivers you.

HOPELESSNESS

Who Really Cares About Me?

In every culture, women carry the domestic burdens of life. Children belong first to mothers. Households are first the responsibility of wives. Making ends meet falls most often to the manager of the home. Centuries of human relationships have not altered the basic facts: Men may be the adventurers and the pioneers, but women move the social fabric forward. They are the backbone of society. And when that backbone is threatened by years of neglect, abuse or discouragement, the foundations of the culture begin to crack. When the value of women diminishes, the society is in serious trouble.

Do you know what it feels like to face insurmountable obstacles day after day, year after year? Do you know that inner desperation that comes when every step reminds you of burdens too heavy to bear? Have you come to the end of yourself, your reserves exhausted, your abilities taxed to the limit, and still have no answer? Those who depend on you will surely suffer. Guilt plagues your mind while pain racks your body. Yet you go on. You must go on. Your life is given to others and they need you to keep walking.

Yeshua encountered a woman who was bent over with life's burdens. Physically, mentally and spiritually, she knew nothing more than the plodding steps of duty. His words changed her life in more ways than one.

The story in Luke 13:10-17

"And when Yeshua saw her, He called her over and said to her, "Woman, you are freed from your sickness." Luke 13:12

How many years does it take to reduce hope to hopelessness? Is there any woman in the world who has not asked that question? How long will I have to endure this disappointing marriage? How long will it take before my children learn to love? How much time will I have to invest before I see a relationship change? How long will I have to endure my illness or my circumstances before God answers? You can add your own situation to the list. Some time along the way, hope gets eaten up and replaced with hopelessness. Life becomes the drudgery on placing one foot in front of another on a road that doesn't end.

On this day, Yeshua met a woman of hopelessness. It doesn't seem as though there is much to this story. It takes only three verses for Luke to relate it. Most of the context seems to point toward the debate of the Pharisees. We never hear about this woman again.

But every life changed by the Savior is worth examining and this woman is no exception.

We know even less about this woman than we discovered about the woman who touched Yeshua's tassels. This pitiful creature had a physical condition that caused her spine to be bent over. She was not able to stand erect at all. For eighteen years she had suffered. Many people tried to help her but without success. This woman's life has become a routine of pain. She has nothing left but the wait for the death.

Even though she is within calling distance of Yeshua, she doesn't look up to see him. She pays no attention to him at all. Why? Because she no longer hopes. After eighteen years of suffering, she is resigned to a life of one foot in front of another. She doesn't seek Yeshua because she no longer believes life can change. She is just like us. Day after day we endure until one day we no longer look up. We just stare at our feet moving forward. We don't see anymore because we live in a world absent of God. We don't even see Him standing right over there.

On this day, she had no idea that God would visit her. She was simply going about her business as best she could. Bent over, crippled, she moved across the portico of the synagogue where Yeshua was teaching, unconscious of everything but her affliction. After all, she could only look up with great effort. Her gazed was fixed on the ground. She knew what it was like to see only her feet.

If we examine the context of this encounter, we see that Yeshua is correcting a theological mistake. This story really starts with a comment on the interpretation of disaster in human life. Yeshua recalls two recent terrible events – the butchering of some Galileans by the Romans and the death of eighteen others through the collapse of a tower. Implied in his remarks is the theology of equal punishment. Yeshua says that just because these disasters befell a certain group, we are not to conclude that these people were more sinful and therefore deserved more punishment. Yeshua corrects this human view of appropriate punishment by telling his audience that unless a man repents, he stands in no better state than any other man and he is equally punishable under God's rule. Then Yeshua adds an illustration that alters the direction of the thought. It is the illustration of God's forbearance and mercy. The fig tree that did not produce was about to be cut down but the gardener asked the owner to wait. And the tree was revived. This is the role Yeshua will play, the one who takes worthless trees and brings them back to life.

As Yeshua concludes this lesson, he sees a crippled woman moving across the square. She is a living illustration of the human view of deserved punishment. And he intends to convert that living illustration into an example of grace. Yeshua sees the plight of this woman. He sees the years of pain burdening her. He sees her inattentive hopelessness. She is a withered fig tree, clinging to a fruitless life. He calls to her.

"Woman, come over here. Come to me."

There is something interesting in this call. The woman was not among the students. For Yeshua to call her, the teaching must stop. But Yeshua does not go to her. She is the cripple and yet he asks her to come to him. I imagine that most of us would have done just the opposite. We would have stopped what we were doing (if we even noticed her) and gone to her side. We would have reasoned, "She is the one who is in pain. I will spare her a few steps of agony and go toward her." But Yeshua does not do this. He remains where he is and asks her to draw closer to him.

Perhaps there is nothing important about this request. Perhaps it is just an accident that the events occurred in this way. But I often pause when something seems a bit odd because I remember the comment of Oswald Chambers:

> The danger with us is that we want to water down the things that Yeshua says and make them mean something in accordance with common sense; if it were only common sense, it was not worthwhile for Him to say it.

Why do you suppose Yeshua asked her to come to him? Do you think that his request might have raised some eyebrows among the students? Do you think that they may have seen this woman as another example of God's punishment for past sins? Do you think they would have been surprised that Yeshua would halt his instruction in order to pay attention to such an insignificant human being?

And what do you imagine she thought? A Rabbi arrests her journey. Does she hesitate to approach him? Does she wonder why he would even care about her? Does she think that she is going to be an object lesson for God's balance scale?

She was certainly acquainted with pity. Eighteen years worth. Luke tells us that for eighteen years no one had been able to help her. Why would she think things would be different today? Nevertheless, she came. She came not expecting anything. She came only because he called. She shuffled to his side, craning her neck upward to see who he was.

That is why Yeshua called her to his side. Yeshua wanted her to "see." He wanted her to look just once more toward God, even if her eyes revealed her hopeless soul. Yeshua asked her to move out of the routine foot-stepping in order to change her perspective. This is the first step in removing hopelessness. Hopelessness is the firm conviction that nothing can change, that the life of despair is bound to continue unrelentingly. And the first step in removing hopelessness is a change in perspective. For this woman, it was as simple as a shift in direction. Yeshua did not go to her because she needed to come to him. She needed to change her direction from the endless foot plodding routine and discover that God was calling her another way.

She did not have to come to Yeshua full of faith. He did not ask her to improve he spirit or find a new self-image. All he asked was this: step away from the usual. Come to me.

There are many plodders in our world. Perhaps you are one of them. Something in your life seems impossible to change. A habit, a responsibility, a failure, a relationship that just hangs on, year after year, until you are worn down, looking only at the ground, following the routine of desperation. *This is the moment God has been waiting for.* God calls us in the middle of hopeless agony. We don't hear him so well when we are walking briskly upright. We need to be bent low before our plodding life pushes us toward hopelessness. And then God says, "Come to me."

Have you heard him calling? Then why are you waiting? If you don't change directions, the road ahead will be just like the road behind. Moving from hopelessness to expectation often involves just the simplest change in direction. Yeshua knows that hope begins with a response to His call. We can always choose to look only at our plodding feet. Or, we can step out of our plodding routine.

When He calls, are you ready to change directions?

Hopelessness (2)

"And when Yeshua saw her, He called her over and said to her, "Woman, you are freed from your sickness." Luke 13:12

This bent-over woman, plodding through a life of hopelessness, turns toward Yeshua. She shuffles to him, simply because he called to her. She expects nothing. Why should she? Many tried, none succeeded. But she responded. And that was enough.

Yeshua did something startling. He laid his hands on her. The word Luke uses for this action is *epitithemi*. This is a compound word made up of two parts – *epi* meaning "upon" and *tithemi*, a verb that means, "to put or set or lay in place." Now this particular verb has an interesting nuance. It is used quite often to mean "to set in the proper order," "to lay a foundation" or "to assign to the proper place." This is exactly what Yeshua is about to accomplish for this woman. With this action he will set her body in the proper order. He will restore the foundation of her spine. He will assign each bone to its proper place. For eighteen years things have been out of order for her. Yeshua is about to restore that order.

The same word, *tithemi*, is used to describe laying down one's life. One day Yeshua will establish another "proper order" by laying down his own life in order to restore the broken back of Mankind. But today, one woman's recovery is enough.

Laying on hands has a long religious history. The hand is often used metaphorically to illuminate God's character. Healing is only one of these metaphors. God places the names of His children on His hands – a reminder that He will never forget us. God's hand protects, provides and guides. The hand is used as a metaphor for God's power and strength. The idea that laying hands on someone as an act of blessing can be found as early as Genesis 48. The physical act that Yeshua performed on that day was not unusual. We are probably justified in believing that many others had tried this method of healing her. What Yeshua did is not surprising. What is surprising is *when* he did it.

This day was the Sabbath. As we soon discover, the Pharisees objected to Yeshua's act not because he performed a miracle of healing but because he performed this "work" on the holy day of rest. No one expected Yeshua to do anything but teach. On the holy day, teaching God's word was acceptable and expected. The crowd listened intently for some new pearl of wisdom. The Pharisees listened just as intently, collecting ammunition to debate his claims. No one paid any attention to a broken down old woman passing by the synagogue. Except Yeshua. He must have startled everyone when he suddenly stopped and called to her. She certainly expected nothing from him. Eighteen years of effort was sufficient evidence that her condition was impossible to cure. And it was the holy day. No one would attempt to deal with a cripple on the holy day. Religious protocol prohibited such foolishness.

Yeshua *invited* the woman to come to him. She could have refused. "Who is this man who makes life even more difficult for me? Doesn't he see I'm crippled? Why should I go to him? He should come to me?" But she went. And when she stepped next to him, he laid his hands on her.

"Woman, you are freed from your sickness." We recognize the opening address. *Gunai*. In Yeshua' mouth, a word of tenderness. A word used to speak to his mother, at the wedding and from the cross. From Yeshua's lips, this broken woman hears a tenderness that she has not known for a long time. She has been used to, "Get out of the way," and "There is nothing I can do for you." She may have overheard, "Look at that poor thing," or "What did she do for God to punish her like that?" But this is not what she hears from Yeshua.

The rest of this phrase is not what we expect. Yeshua is healing a deformity of the spine. We expect, "you are **healed** from your sickness." But Yeshua uses a word that implies bondage, not illness. He literally says that she has been let free. The Greek verb is *apolutrosis*. What it really means is so important that it changes everything about this verse. This Greek verb is about paying a ransom in order to free a slave or prisoner. It is the word for redemption. It is a word from the slave market. Yeshua is not *healing* this woman. He is *redeeming* her from the bondage of Satan.

Yeshua is still teaching. But now he is teaching with a demonstration of the power of God. In order to understand exactly what he is teaching, we have to look at the word for "sickness."

The Greek word *astheneia* is generally the word for weakness. It also is used for illness. It can be related to the entire person or to a specific condition that results in weakness to the body. Some Pharisees taught that pious fulfillment of the law resulted in good health and material prosperity. Conversely, sin produced the punishment of illness and poverty. Yeshua was about to demonstrate the fallacy of this doctrine. By healing this woman with a proclamation that she was being loosed from bondage, Yeshua implied that her illness was not the result of God's judgment but rather the work of Satan. Yeshua affirmed that this illness was evil. It was not part of God's intention for men or women. In fact, in the discussion that follows, Yeshua specifically tells the objecting Pharisees that this woman had been *bound* by Satan all of these years. On this day, Yeshua fulfills one of the functions of the messianic announcement from Isaiah 61. He releases a captive.

Matthew 8:17 uses this word to describe one of the functions of the Savior. Quoting Isaiah 53:4, Matthew says that Christ took our weakness upon himself. His saving power embraces much more than our sins. That power reaches into every part of who we are.

Yeshua demonstrated the authority and the mission of the Messiah on this day. God's power reached into this woman's life and redeemed her from Satan's grip on her body. There is no mention of forgiveness. There is no request for repentance. This action is a demonstration of God's intention to release His children from the chains that bind them *simply because God is merciful*. Mercy is in His nature.

If we reflect the character of Yeshua, we will display mercy *without prior expectation*. Yeshua's action revealed the nature of the Father. We are called to do the same. When His calling reaches you and you come to Him, you rediscover hope. Are you calling to others who are shuffling the paths of hopelessness? If they respond, are you pouring out mercy without conditions?

Hopelessness (3)

"And when Yeshua saw her, He called her over and said to her, "Woman, you are freed from your sickness." Luke 13:12

Call and response. The preamble to change. Then active engagement. After eighteen years of human failure, God straightens life out with a simple touch. Mercy given and received. The woman is healed and freed. The bonds are broken. What next?

The story moves on. Yeshua issues a challenge to the Pharisees' hypocrisy. The woman disappears from the pages. But not before we learn one more thing. She glorified God. The verb is *doxazo*. It is the root of our word "doxology." The important element is the verb tense. It is in the imperfect tense. This is continuous or repeated action in the past. For eighteen years this woman suffered the painful, shame-filled life of a cripple. For eighteen years Satan bound her body in hideous chains. And now, for the rest of her life, she will continuously glorify God. She has been released.

Today we have medical treatment for scoliosis and spinal disorders. Our cripples are aesthetically usually hidden from society. After all, in our culture only perfect bodies will do. We feed ourselves with digitally reconstructed images of youthful pride. In the process, we rob ourselves of the opportunity to glorify God continuously. We begin to think that unless we have lives of upright magnificence, we have nothing to offer, not even to God. On this day, Yeshua reversed all the beliefs that God helps those who help themselves. He overturned all the cherished theology that health and wealth are the result of blessings and poverty and disease the result of punishment. On this day, Yeshua smashed the ritual that confined God to Man's religious box. On this day, Yeshua redeemed one of God's own.

In this story, we will identify with either the woman or the listeners. We will either see that our infirmities are the opportunity for God's glory or we will secretly ask, "Why should she get the benefit of God's grace when I am so much more deserving?" We will be the ones who ask nothing more of life than seeing feet and discover that life is about praise to God, or we will be the ones who have often proclaimed His majesty but confine God's grace to our acceptable boxes.

This woman received more than an upright posture. She received a constant motivation for thankfulness. Her life became the seedbed of glorifying the God who touched her. Mercy leads to praise.

Yeshua came to loose every woman bound by the power of Satan. The Scripture tells us that He took our weaknesses on Himself in order to release us from captivity. What binds you today? Where is the hopelessness of your life? What bends your back with its heavy load? What keeps you looking at the ground when God wants you to raise your eyes to heaven? If you come when He calls, He will lay His hands on you and say, "Woman, you have been set free."

REJECTION

Do you see me?

If love is what we all want, rejection is what we all fear. There is nothing quite as damaging as being told that you don't belong. "Don't bother me. Can't you see I'm busy?" "What are you doing here anyway?" "Who told you to come? You're not welcome." You can add your own variations to the theme from your life story. Somewhere along the way we have all felt the cold sting of dismissal. Sometime in our past we knew the flash of shame that comes when we weren't welcome. If the world needs love, it has a very strange way of showing it.

In what must be one of the strangest stories of the Gospels, Yeshua deals with rejection. But he seems to be on the wrong side of the equation. He seems to be handing out the dismissal, shunning someone in desperate need. Is Yeshua really this callous, this demeaning? The story compels us to look deeper, to find a way inside the window in order to *feel* the emotions released in this encounter. What does the heart of God have to say when we feel as though we have been pushed away, even by Him?

The story in Matthew 15:21-28

"O woman, your faith is great; be it done for you as you wish."
Matthew 15:28

Turned away! Worse than that. Not only turned back but rejected. "Not good enough for God's care." This is not what we expect from Yeshua. How could he turn away someone in need?

The story is a difficult one to understand. We have this image of Yeshua as the one who accepts everyone, who is always available and is never harsh to the humble or desperate. But when we read this account in Matthew, we are struck by his remarks. They seem so cruel. His actions seem to tell this woman, "Don't bother me. I did not come to minister to you."

This is a traveling tale. Yeshua and the disciples are walking toward Tyre and Sidon. A woman approaches the group, crying out in a loud voice, "Lord, Son of David, have pity on me!" Unfortunately, she is one of the outcasts. Matthew tells us that her ethnic background is Canaanite. But by New Testament times, the country once known as Canaan no longer existed. This reference is to ethnic lineage, not political association. It is exactly the situation that exists in the Middle East today. There is no country called Palestine, yet everyone knows those who call themselves Palestinians. This designation tells us not about their nationalism but about their heritage. For Matthew, the designation Canaanite meant only one critical thing – outside of the acceptable community of God's chosen. This woman did not belong. She did not belong to the house of Israel (as Yeshua clearly indicates), she did not belong to the nation of Canaan (since it did not exist) and she did not belong in the company of the Messiah of the Jews.

When she begins her wailing appeals, Yeshua does not respond. The text does not say that he ignored her. It says only that he did not answer. But the disciples react. They are upset and annoyed. They do not appreciate the aggravation she is causing in spite of her need. In fact, they turn a deaf ear to the brokenhearted attempt of this woman to find help for her child. They tell Yeshua to send her away. They respond to the obvious. She does not belong with us. Tell her to go away.

This woman broke more than ethnic protocol. She came unaccompanied by her husband. This could mean she did not have a husband. In any event, no single woman should have engaged in conversation with a group of men. And she brought along a curse – her daughter. In this culture, a demon-possessed child was a clear indication of God's punishment for sin. This woman was defiled. Finally, she was not socially polite. She made noise. She pleaded. She carried on. This woman did not know her place.

She is the equivalent of the modern refugee. She has no country, no tribe. Since she comes to Yeshua without a husband, we can assume that she is alone in the world. She has only her cursed daughter. Everything is against her. But she hears that Yeshua is coming, Yeshua the healer, Yeshua who shows compassion on the desperate, Yeshua who brings a new kingdom. So she risks it all to put herself before him.

You are walking along the street with several friends. It is a pleasant day in the city and soon you will be enjoying good conversation over a great meal at the nearby restaurant. But as you and your friends pass by the alley, you see the pitiful sight of a homeless mother with her child. For one brief moment, your eyes lock. As though her eyes suddenly become yours, you see what she sees – the chosen ones, passing through life as though God's favor belongs only to them, ignoring the plight of a mother who has known only sorrow. The flash of identity passes. But the woman in rags knows. She steps forward. "Please, please help me. My little girl is sick. I have nothing to feed her. Won't you help us?"

Jesus Said To Her

The matted hair, the dirty face, the smell, the voice – an emotional assault that catches you off guard. You were thinking about a nice lunch and good company when your world confronted this outsider. You fight between panic and pity. You want to get away but her words tug at your heart. You did not come to minister to the homeless today. You aren't dressed for it.

Your friends push you forward. "Oh, that's disgusting. How can people allow themselves to live like that? There must be a shelter or somewhere she can go." As they try to urge you along, you see the woman following. She is crying.

"You know, you just can't be sure. If you give her something, how do you know she won't just buy drugs? I hear that's all they really want anyway." But the woman cries out, "Please, lady, help me." Now you realize that she is young. The time on the street has aged her. She could be your child. Children bearing children. You wonder about the tiny body clutched in her arms. Was it really a child, or just a doll? Your steps falter.

"Look, just send her away." One of your friends touches you reassuringly on the arm. "We can't have her following us like this. Everyone will stare! It's embarrassing."

Come with me to Cite Soleil in the port district of Port-au-Prince, Haiti. 300,000 people living on a 2 square mile garbage dump. Water so polluted that it smells. Open sewers run like the tentacles of a diseased monster. And children. Everywhere. Digging for scraps. Flies covering their faces. Bellies swollen from malnutrition. Slowly dying. By the thousands. Once noted as the poorest place in the Western hemisphere, Cite Soleil has a new badge. It is now the most dangerous place in the Western hemisphere. Rape, murder, robbery, beatings and every other kind of violence is an everyday way of life here. 245 miles from South Beach, 7 million people are starving to death in Haiti while the glittering crowds of south Florida drink $9 martinis and eat $100 dinners. These are the outcasts, rounded up and put into the concentration camp of the global economy. Surrounded by a prison of bright blue water, they have nothing to offer the world except the cry of their need. And the world does not respond to need unless there is something to gain. So, tip the valet parking attendant and drive away in your new Lexus. There is no reason at all to think about Cite Soleil.

The first step in understanding this encounter with Yeshua is acknowledging which role we play. Are we the socially annoyed or the clamoring needy? Are we the righteous or the refugees? This is a story about personal pride. It is a story about who matters. Unless we stand with the Canaanite woman, Yeshua will be nothing more than the leader of the acceptable. God's grace falls on outcasts of the world because they know their need. To lead like Yeshua is to see our outcast faces in the mirror, accepted only because He cares.

Yeshua encountered a refugee on this trip to Tyre. This outsider cries out, "Son of David, help my daughter." The Greek word that describes her cry is onomatopoetic. It makes its own sound. *Krauge*. The sound of a cry. The crying of an old crow. Caw. Caw. The annoying sound designed for only one purpose – to get attention. *Krauge, krauge*. But Yeshua does not respond.

How do you get God's attention when you have nothing but your need? This woman teaches us a great lesson. Need is enough. She does not stand on protocol. She does not consider the consequences. She does not wait for the right setting, the right attitude or the right contact. She "caws" after God. She steps boldly forward and makes her need known. She has no other way. On every other basis, she is excluded. But need overcomes all other reasons. When women are consumed with the needs of their children, nothing stands in the way. Not pride, not protocol, not personality. They will go to any lengths to provide what their children need. Perhaps that's why God often asks us to take the role of the protective mother. Perhaps that's why He describes Himself in the same role. Perhaps we need to come to God in the same way that mother's protect their children. Would that make a difference to you?

Is your need so great that you are ready to set aside all other expectations? Do the pangs of desperation twist you with such hurt that you count nothing important except a word from the Lord? We would all do well to enter into the role of the refugee. We are people without a nation, a home or a heritage until God finds us. Don't let anything get in the way of your need for Him. Not even when He doesn't answer. God has something important in mind, even in His silence. Keep cawing.

Rejection (2)

"O woman, your faith is great; be it done for you as you wish."
Matthew 15:28

The refugee woman "caws" in her desperation. "Have pity on me, Son of David." Her plea is not accidental. The title she uses (Son of David) says something important. This title was associated with the expected Messiah. The expected *Jewish* Messiah. But this woman does not belong to the people of the Messiah. She knows that she does not belong. So she uses an official title that means, "I believe that you are the Jewish Messiah, the expected one. Won't you have pity on me even though I am an outcast?" Perhaps she did know her place. It was the place of exclusion.

Some commentators suggest that her initial attempt to engage Yeshua was based on a deliberate manipulation using this Jewish title. She tried to sway Yeshua by placating him with these words. But there is no indication in the text that she was not completely sincere. Yeshua often encountered people outside the Jewish religious community who recognized who he really was. In fact, more often than not those who did not share the restricting presuppositions of the Jews were able to see the truth. There is no reason to claim that this woman did not see Yeshua as the hoped for Messiah. She sees who He is. Will He see who she is?

Matthew describes her appeal with the word *eleeo* – mercy. But the Greek thought behind this word is not at all what Yeshua taught about mercy. In the Greek culture, mercy was not a moral or legal consideration. It was a psychological emotional response. We are swept into the emotion of mercy when we come into contact with someone who is experiencing *undeserved* suffering. Something in us responds to the plight of another. We just can't help it. And this creates another problem in the Greek mind. Mercy is connected with *fear*. Since there is no apparent reason for this tragedy, it reminds us that tragedy could also happen to us. Mercy is not a passion that is aroused when we see someone suffering because they deserved it. We don't feel sorry for them. Actions have consequences. If they are suffering because of justified consequences, then that is right. No mercy is required. But *undeserved suffering* is another story. It creates the fear of "what if."

As you approach the restaurant, the homeless child with a child catches up to your group. She reaches for your sleeve. Do you feel panic? Are you afraid? Does the emotional response of her misery make you shudder? Your friends quickly push her aside.

"Go away. Leave us alone or we'll call the police." Protection.

"You should be ashamed of yourself! Why don't you go to a shelter?" Guilt.

But you can't move. There is something else here besides fear and justice.

In the Old Testament, mercy is an obligation of a covenant promise. The stronger party shows mercy to the weaker party. That means giving help to one who is in need. Mercy is a reflection of God's help toward His people. Mercy demonstrates God's love for His own creation. God loved us before He made promises to us. In fact, His help toward us did not depend on our keeping the terms of the promise. God desired to rain His love and compassion on us when we needed it most, after we have broken our relationship with Him, while we were excluded.

Mercy is the *act* of benevolence toward the one in need. It is not sympathy. It is not social responsibility. It is my hand lifting your hand. It is personally involved compassion. Because mercy is part of the fabric of the covenant, it is not a sign of weakness. In fact, mercy demonstrates God's strength. He is so powerful that He is able to release us from punishment without compromising the Law. How He does this is the story of the crucifixion.

Yeshua knew that mercy is about sacrifice. It is about the sacrifice of making choices. The Greeks were wrong. The emotion of mercy, the overwhelming disturbance of the soul when we are confronted with one like us who is tormented, is not something to be avoided. Life is designed to bring us face-to-face with sorrow and grief. There is a reason for this: God wants us to see our real status in His court. But the Greeks did not have a personal Creator and Judge behind their philosophy. They only had Law. So, being merciful made them afraid. It reminded them that life is ultimately uncontrollable. Without a sovereign God, anything can happen. No matter how many laws men make, the world doesn't behave accordingly. So, every time I feel the call of mercy, I recognize that I'm not in control – and I'm afraid. Those who cannot abide the cost of mercy do all they can to avoid the confrontation with pain.

Mercy is the summary word of the life of Yeshua. He made a very costly choice. He gave up being God to be like God's enemies – one of us. And mercy cost God too. He lost His only son to the sacrifice for those who deserved to die. Punishing Yeshua for our sins cost God the Father the unfathomable sorrow of seeing rejection spewed on someone He loved forever. A person who didn't deserve any of God's wrath. To show mercy is always expensive.

This woman cawing at Yeshua was not asking for sympathy. She was asking for sacrifice. She was asking for the Son of David to sacrifice the *expected role* of the *Jewish* Messiah and see her as a creature of God worth loving.

This woman shows us the power of need. But it is not need alone that will rescue her. Need will keep her prisoner until need encounters compassion. Yeshua demonstrates God's view of compassion. Compassion means sacrifice. We are not compassionate when we give from our wealth. That act might be generous, but it misses the critical element of compassion. We are compassionate when the gift is a sacrifice, just as God's gift was a sacrifice. Mercy is my willingness to forego what is rightfully mine in order that someone else may benefit. Mercy costs!

If you come to God in great need, remember the great cost of His answer. He is more than willing to pay the price for you. When you accept His compassion, are you willing to bear the cost for some else? You will never become like Yeshua until you count the cost of grace for another. This woman demonstrates godly compassion. She does not plead for herself. What indignities she must near do not matter. She pleads for another. She empties herself for another. She shows that she is willing to endure whatever it takes to gain mercy for another. And *that* is God's way!

Rejection (3)

"O woman, your faith is great; be it done for you as you wish."
Matthew 15:28

"Send her away." She has no case. Her lot is her just reward. She is not one of us. We have no obligation to her. And, on top of all that, she is too annoying. Caw. Caw.

Yeshua does not answer her cawing because He is waiting to see this drama played out. The disciples are in full costume – the proper heritage, the proper company, the proper affront. They demand the proper response.

It is not clear if Yeshua speaks to the disciples or to the woman or both. But it is clear that he establishes the boundary of the sacrifice.

"I was sent only to the lost sheep of the house of Israel." The word "only" is the translation of the combination of *ei* with *me*. Other passages in Matthew that use this combination are translated "except," "but only" or "if not". This could give us, "I was not sent *except* to the lost sheep . ." or "I was not sent *if not* to the lost sheep . ." But maybe there is another way to look at this remark.

There is virtually no punctuation in the oldest Greek texts. The intonation and sentence structure must often be determined by the context. A question in Greek is not identified by a particular mark like "?". It is a matter of context. There is no change in word order in Greek to indicate a question. What if Yeshua is asking a question rather than making a statement? "Was I not sent only to the lost sheep of the house of Israel?"

Context must determine the structure. The parallel passage in Mark (7:24-30) does not include this statement. Therefore, we have only the context of Matthew to guide us. We know that Matthew focused his gospel on Jewish issues. The phrase "house of Israel" is a Jewish expression describing God's chosen people. But this raises a dilemma. The phrase may be understood from the perspective of nationalism or from the perspective of faith. Nationalism implies Yeshua's mission is only to those who are in the bloodline of Abraham. Some commentators say, "His mission therefore was exclusively to God's chosen people Israel."[4]

But Yeshua does not seem to have acted according to this restriction. He deals with the Roman Centurion, the Samaritan woman and her entire village and other Gentiles. In fact, he often commends the faith of these people with greater praise than the faith found among the Jews (Matt. 8:5-13). Furthermore, Paul makes it clear that God never intended an exclusive nationalism but rather a lineage based on faith. One of the principal themes of Matthew is Yeshua's constant attack on the thinking that God was the exclusive property of Jewish descent. Therefore, we must reject this interpretation. Matthew is anxious to show Yeshua as the true Messiah, not for those of Jewish blood but for those who have put their faith in the one true God. Deliverance comes *through* the Jews but it is not limited to the Jews.

The other interpretation of the phrase "house of Israel" points to the children of God who are His children by faith, not by birth. This "house" encompasses the true Israel and includes all who come by faith, regardless of national or genetic background.

---

[4] R.V. G. Tasker, *The Gospel According to St. Matthew*, (Eerdmans, 1973), p. 150.

And this is precisely the point of our story. Yeshua uses this circumstance to once again draw attention to the prejudice of the Jews, in this case, his own disciples. They viewed the "house of Israel" from the perspective of bloodline. This woman was not included. But Yeshua may be challenging this thought in a rather unique way.

"Was I not sent only to the lost sheep of the house of Israel?"

As a question, the force of this interaction turns the focus on the disciples. They have certainly decided that this refugee is *not part of God's household*? As a question, Yeshua raises the issue of their presuppositions about God. The question demands an answer. Is it true or not? And the answer reveals the presupposition about God's house. Yeshua has proposed a test case for group inclusion. Will his disciples see who can be included in the "lost sheep"? Or will they continue to live with ethnic and cultural blinders?

This woman sees the opening, a way to be counted among the lost sheep. Yeshua provides the opening by asking the implied question, "Who are the lost sheep?" She responds by worshipping Him. The act of falling on her face, of being prostrate before him, is the obeisance of a dog before its master. The gesture is not lost on Yeshua. It is as if she said, "I am one of the lost sheep, Son of David. I prove my inclusion by worshipping you as the One sent from God." She repeats her desperate appeal. "Lord, help me." The word she uses is sharp and direct. It means to run to give assistance. Lord, come running to me to give me aid. Don't wait. I need it now.

There is a day in your life when your need overpowers you. Inside or outside the circle of social acceptance, you have to fall before the Lord of life and say, "Lord, please include me. I have nothing more than my need, but all that I have I offer in worship to You. Please let me in."

That day changes a life forever. It moves us from refugee to citizen. It alters our perspective on every other "unacceptable" one. We know what it is like to see from the outside. Our encounters with the refugees of life become open doors or mercy. We once stood on the other side too. May God help us to never forget – we are the accepted refugees.

Rejection (4)

"O woman, your faith is great; be it done for you as you wish."
Matthew 15:28

Yeshua puts the test before her once again. "It is not good to take the children's bread and throw it to the dogs." Carefully, carefully Yeshua directs the drama. "It is not *good*." The word is *kalos*. *Kalos* has a wide range of meanings from "morally virtuous" to "harmonious and beautiful." In this particular case, the combination of "is not good" means "is not useful or profitable." There is no *moral* implication here. It is simply a statement about advantage or gain. In other words, Yeshua places one more test before his audience. "There is nothing gained by taking what is intended for the children and throwing it to the dogs."

The dog-woman is not asking for a place at the table. She has come to Yeshua seeking his compassion. Anything will do. Notice that Yeshua is not refusing her request. He is not saying she is outside what is morally right to do. He is presenting a different obstacle: there is nothing to gain here. Why, implies Yeshua, should I do this for you? What is in it for me? She can't barter for his favor because she has nothing useful to exchange.

Her answer is the answer of faith. "Yes, Lord," is the phrase of agreement. "Yes, I know that I have nothing to offer." "Yes, I know that you are the Messiah of the Jews, not of my people." "Yes, I know that I don't belong." "Yes, Lord, I know that there is no gain for you." "I agree with all that you have said, Lord." "But those with nothing to offer are willing to accept what is of no use to others." Crumbs from the table.

Return with me to Cite Soleil. Cardboard boxes. Worn out shipping containers. Rusty barrels. Crumbs from the world's table. Useless. But for those with nothing, these crumbs are shelter. There are tens-of-thousands of people living in cardboard boxes, old barrels and useless containers. There are piles of cast off rags and worn out shoes – clothing for the dog-people of Haiti. In a world of left-behinds, nothing is wasted. Every single scrap finds a use.

Your friends push you toward the restaurant door.

"You can't help her, you know. Look at her. She has nothing to offer you – except maybe that you'll get some awful disease."

"You know what will happen if you give her money. She'll want more. They always do."

"Why don't we just call a shelter or something? They have people who do this sort of thing. It's not up to us. After all, how can we be expected to deal with this? We're not prepared."

But the explanation and justification fades into the background. You stop. Even the young girl is caught off guard. You take a step toward her and grasp her hands. There are two people crying now.

"Oh, my child. How can I help you today?"

It's not about advantage. It's not about gain. It's not about "right" or "proper." It's about compassion. It's about a God who had no reason to give Himself to those worthless creatures who despoiled His creation and their own lives. It's about the God-Man who died for the dogs. It's about recognizing need without calculating loss.

Blessed are the merciful because they are willing to pay the price of being compassionate.

"Oh, woman, your faith is great." You, my dog-woman, know the secret of need. You know that God's heart is open to all of the lost children of His house. You know that He has a special place for the useless and abused and left-out. You know that God cares for those who have only need. He is the God of life's refugees – you and me.

REMORSE

Can I forgive myself?

What happens when we experience the emotional destruction of remorse? How do we feel when we suddenly realize that our lives have been wasted in selfish pursuit or useless pleasure? How do we react when we confront the shame of who we have been?

Yeshua lived and worked among the outcasts of society. He spent his time with the sick, the defiled, the unacceptable, the fearful and the dangerous. Among those who found no solace in the human community, Yeshua became a magnet of validation. He gave people hope. He restored their shattered images. And in the process, he encountered more than one who crashed into the wall of shame.

Most of us have learned the social etiquette of concealing our shame. We engage in repentance and plead for forgiveness within the confines of the acceptable. We cloak the real rupture in our souls. But once in awhile we experience what it really means to be rescued from the pit within us. Once in awhile we are empowered to pull back the curtain of social propriety and let the dam of human degradation break into the light. When that happens, our shame spills into this religiously proper world like a flood of polluted water. That's when we need a real soul-healer. That's when polite and proper religious authorities speak words without impact. But a man or woman who allows us to cry, oh, that's a welcomed friend.

The story of Luke 7:36-50

"And He said to the woman, "Your faith has saved you; go in peace." Luke 7:50

She could not have been more than eighteen. She was not remarkably attractive. She had tattoos and scars in the wrong places. She stammered a bit. She wasn't tall enough to reach the microphone. But this frail young woman brought tears to the eyes of every one of the 600 people who listened in silent awe. Her story was the story of Luke 7.

Melanie grew up in a difficult home. Between unemployment and alcohol, her parents managed to stay together just long enough to get her into high school. Then her father left for good. Depression pushed Melanie toward drugs. Within months she was a steady customer of the local supplier. She didn't always have money. But she had something else he wanted. He took it whenever the mood struck him. By 16, Melanie was pregnant, hooked, sick and desperate. And no one cared.

She lived on the streets, surviving by selling herself, trying to conceal her growing abdomen so that she could attract customers. She got hepatitis and ended up in the county hospital. No one came to visit her. The baby died before it was born. On the day she was released, she took her first overdose. But she made a mistake. It didn't kill her.

With tears streaming down her face, Melanie talked to the same crowd that never saw her walking in the alleys, never knew she was sleeping in doorways, never watched her hunting through their garbage cans. Now, standing before the audience in this Florida upscale beach side church, she exposed the shame of her life – and the power of God to find those who have been forgotten.

"I just wanted to die, but somehow I couldn't make it work. Then one day a lady found me sitting on the curb by her shop. I looked horrible. She just said one thing to me. Nobody said that to me for a long time. She just said, "Why don't you let me help you?" I just cried and cried. She sat right there on the street and held me. I was a mess. I asked her, "Why do you care?" and she said to me, "Let me tell you what Yeshua did for me."

When Melanie finished her brief testimony, she received a standing ovation. The preacher hugged her and said that there would be no sermon today. Nothing he could say would speak of God's love more than this. He was right. God found Melanie and brought her home.

Two thousand years earlier, Yeshua went to the house of Simon for dinner. Simon was an important man of the community. A religious leader. A powerful figure. But the dinner did not go as Simon planned. A young woman with a terrible past interrupted the meal. God found her and brought her home to Yeshua.

Simon's dinner party was not a private affair. Simon loved his importance and power. Yeshua appeared to be on the rise, so Simon invited him to a meal. In all likelihood, Simon the Pharisee wished to get a close look at this new prophet named Yeshua. But Simon was not interested in Yeshua's message. He was probably more interested in trapping Yeshua in order to establish his own superiority. For this reason, Simon invited Yeshua but he failed to act as host (as we shall see).

Unfortunately, Simon's desire for personal power left the door open for something else. It was not uncommon in this culture for uninvited people to gather around a meal of important figures. These people became the audience of the play, watching the center stage for entertainment and education. But today a woman of the streets got into the house. This took incredible courage. Not only was she forbidden to enter, by doing so she brought defilement on those within the house. And even more outrageously, she did not keep her place in the background but moved up to the reclining men and stood behind Yeshua.

This woman (shall we call her Melanie?) brought with her a very expensive alabaster jar of perfume. Overcome with remorse, shattered by forgiveness, she stood behind Yeshua who was stretched out next to the low table of food. She began to cry. She couldn't help it. The tears just wouldn't stop. Sobs racked her body. She groaned. This man had changed her life. No more "tricks." No more secrets. God visited her and freed her from the bondage of her need and her shame. She cried over a life that might have been, a life that had been thrown away and most of all, for a life beginning again.

The tears cascaded down her cheeks and fell like rain on Yeshua's feet. Two thousand years before the lyrics were written, "The sky is crying. Just see the tears roll down the street," each drop left a tiny circle in the dust. Yeshua never moved. It was sweet rain, born from the clouds of repentance.

But Simon was not so happy. He thought to himself, "This rabbi, Yeshua, isn't all that I thought he was. If he were really a prophet as they claim, he would know that this street tramp is a worthless piece of sinful trash. He would never let her get close to him, let alone touch him. He is being defiled by her and she is defiling my house." Simon is a prisoner of his inherited chauvinism at the same time that he is a perpetrator of sinful behavior toward God's greatest creation.

Before we can see the tender passion in this story, we must see the harsh criticism and censure. This window looks in on a life of public pride. Simon was a man who could not recognize remorse and regret because he could not recognize his own failure. Before we can stand behind Yeshua and weep, we must stand in front of Him and wail. "My sin is ever before me" is the basis of tears of repentance. Yeshua is for us much more than the forgiving God-man. He is the brilliant light exposing my darkest deeds. Only when I see who I really am in His light will I be able to shed the tears of change.

If you have never stood behind him crying, perhaps it's because you have never let him expose your deepest self. Your expression of gratitude is the reciprocal of the depth of your sin. Where there is little awareness of failure, there is little need for tears. Have you allowed Yeshua to show you who you really are today? Are the tears of heaven rolling down your street?

Remorse (2)

"And He said to the woman, "Your faith has saved you; go in peace." Luke 7:50

The woman bent down and began to wipe Yeshua's feet with her hair. Still the tears fell. She took the perfume and poured it over his feet. Wiping, sobbing, then kissing them.

Simon turned away. It was disgusting. How could this supposed teacher of righteousness allow such a disgraceful act? Why, it was almost as bad as using her! The thought made him shudder. He had no appetite now.

Luke carefully crafts the scene. We miss some of the nuances in English translations. The first Technicolor word is "weeping." "and standing behind *Him*, weeping" uses the Greek verb *klaio*. This is a verb that describes the wailing and lamenting at a funeral. It is not silent shedding of tears. It is demonstrative groaning, agonizing and sobbing. It is associated with death and grief. It is Melanie standing at the microphone, choking on her tears. Simon is disgusted because the woman not only defiles his house and his guest, she makes a scene of it all. She is loud. She is a spectacle. She is a whore wailing in his front room. His carefully orchestrated prestige party is turning into a nightmare. What will the townspeople remember now? That some street hooker took over the stage?

The next image is about her hair. According to Rabbinic law, it was shameful for a woman to let her hair down in a public place. This woman's sacrifice brings shame on herself and on Yeshua as she uses her hair to wipe the dust and tears from his feet. Her hair becomes the towel of a slave kneeling before the master. She knows nothing except his forgiveness. No cultural inhibition can restrain her emotion. The mixture of tears, perfume and the scent of her hair fill the room. She is uninhibited in her display of devotion. And it is her reckless gratitude that grates on Simon.

Her final act of impropriety is a kiss. Another Technicolor word. *Kataphileo*. This is not a simple kiss of acknowledgment. It is not the "peck on the cheek" when you greet a friend (if you happen to be Italian). Luke adds the prefix *kata* for emphasis and intensity. This sign was recognized as a symbol of intense and deep affection. This is repeated adoration. Her kisses are unbridled remorse and unrestrained joy. This woman is worshipping her deliverer.

When Melanie left the platform in that beachside church, there was rejoicing. The strongest men were wiping their eyes. The women were shaking with sobs. Forgiveness is the world's most powerful medicine. It is God's miracle drug. One dose can change everything about life. The difference between men and women in emotional reaction to Melanie's story is worthy of reflection. Why did the women sob while the men tried to hold back tears? What cultural forces have prevented men from experiencing the shattering broken-heartedness of hope recovered? Why are women able to enter into this experience without restraint while men find it torturously difficult?

Have you experienced the unspeakable joy of forgiveness? Have you let go of the social protocol, the expectations, the fear and the shame to show your Savior what forgiveness means to you? Have you stood behind Him, unable to control the mixture of sorrow and joy, while tears from heaven washed His feet? Perhaps one of the reasons that this woman and Melanie touch us so deeply is that we also wish to stand before the world and proclaim our freedom from guilt. We *need* to cry tears from heaven. But so often we stand in the crowd, hearts in agreement but feet firmly planted. Yeshua spent most of His ministry hunting for those who were desperate for love because out of desperation comes action. Until we see our own desperation, we will never know the bitter cleansing of the tears of repentance or the savor of the tears of forgiveness.

There are two common denominators among all people – pain and calling. My pain is not just my suffering in life. It is the pain I foisted upon God when I made myself the king of my life. Until I see my own destruction, I will not feel His redemption. But when I truly confront my pain, I discover a call. It is the call of the kiss – to embrace those in the agony of living without Him and shower them with tears of joy.

If you discover that your expression of worship is constrained by your fear of others, you need to remember the woman in Simon's house. Yeshua rejoiced with her because she knew nothing but grace. She had no shame before men because she had no shame before God. She sets the stage for each of us. Have you left your shame behind in the tears on the floor?

Remorse (3)

"And He said to the woman, "Your faith has saved you; go in peace." Luke 7:50

Yeshua knew Simon's attitude. So he presented Simon with a parable. It is a story about the relationship between debt and gratitude. Yeshua describes two men who both owe debts. One owes a small amount, the other a very large amount. Neither can pay. But the creditor decides to show both of them mercy and forgives all that is due. Then Yeshua says to Simon, "Which one of these men do you suppose will show the most gratitude?" Simon, being no financial fool, answers correctly. The man with the greatest debt. But Simon's answer betrays him. He knows the moral that's coming so he replies, *"I suppose the one whom he forgave more."*

Isn't sarcasm grand? It says so much about the speaker. With just a word of sarcasm you can turn truth into pain, intimacy into fear or vulnerability into resistance. It's such a useful tool. It takes almost no training to become an expert in this field. All you have to do is open your mouth and let what's already there come out.

His answer, "I suppose" is acknowledgement with an edge. Yes, if you insist. But it doesn't apply to *me*. I am righteous. I live by the rules.

The word *hupolambano* combines the thought of "being under" with "taking." It is as if to say, "I'll take it under consideration. I'll think about it." It is a condescending agreement. "Yes, Yeshua. You made your point." This is acknowledgment without commitment for Simon the Pharisee does not admit that he is the one who stands convicted before God. He is acting the part of the defense lawyer. "Objection sustained." A point given but only a technicality. In his world, the category "sinner" is a brand that could never apply to him.

Where do we stand in this courtroom? Are we alongside the woman, admitted sinners, aware of our guilt and shame? Or are we holding on to the technicality, admitting nothing that would drive us to our knees to beg forgiveness? It's so easy to see those "others" as the sinners they are. It's not so easy to see our own reflection in God's mirror.

If you haven't wept over your sin, how can you weep over God's forgiveness?
Simon's attitude is the lightening bolt of condemnation. Even in his affirmation, he is aloof from remorse and repentance.

Then Yeshua turns toward this woman whose reputation has preceded her. He says, "When I entered your home, Simon, you did not offer me the common courtesy of a guest. You did not give me water to wash my feet. You did not greet me with a kiss. You did not anoint my head with oil. But this woman is expressing her gratitude in all these things, not because she was obliged to do so but because a great debt that has been forgiven."

In one sense, Simon and this woman were exactly the same. They were both debtors before God. But the woman recognized her need. She faced her own history without denial or excuse or justification. When forgiveness came, the monumental burden she carried was removed. Gratitude overwhelmed her. She could not help demonstrating her love.

You and I are likely to be seduced into the role of Simon. We aren't really *that* bad. We have all made mistakes, of course. But our debts are small. So small that they really don't amount to much. They're just technicalities. And so our gratitude is withheld. We fail to see the incredible cost of the sacrifice to redeem us because we minimize the debt instead of recognizing the generosity of the creditor. We miss the tenderness of tears of joy because we will not submit to the pain of repentance. Like Simon, we are bound by our own motives and rules. We concede the point instead of embracing the gift.

It is such a tragedy. God stands ready to forgive all our debts. Yet we hold back. We find it so amazingly difficult to admit what we know to be true about ourselves. We are not likely to stand in front of the congregation and tell the depths of our stories. And so, we do not experience the immense relief of God's forgiveness. We give Him only what we imagine are the "acceptable" mistakes and we go on carrying the burdens of guilt and shame for our secrets.

Yeshua has two things to say to those who acknowledge themselves as debtors before the throne of God. The first is the confirmation of God's act of grace: "Your sins are forgiven." He grants us freedom from our shame. He removes the penalty of our debt. For this, we fall before Him in worship.

The word "forgiven" is a word that in its earliest examples meant "to let go" or "to release." It was widely used for the remission of a debt. With this word, Yeshua applies his parable to the woman standing before him. Her debt is remitted. But more than a debt is struck off the books. The Old Testament influence on this word shaped it to fit the idea of God's removal of the defilement of sin. Yeshua' announcement in the presence of Simon the Pharisee points directly to the Scriptural basis of forgiveness. Only God can forgive. Forgiveness does not occur by human illumination, pious behavior or ritual practice. It is a gift of God that can only be received by those who concur with God's judgment about their lives. The only difference between this woman and Simon is God's intervention.

"Your sins are remitted" is a proclamation that her life has been transformed from shame and guilt to acceptance because God says so. It is not just her past that has been washed away. God's declaration is the overthrow of sin's power in human life – a power that rules every aspect of existence until His mercy arrives.

This statement is a shock to Simon – and to us. Not because we retain the Pharisaic culture of the first century, but because this forgiveness is reckless.[5] Yeshua does not supply her with the "conditions" of her debt cancellation. He doesn't offer an instructional course in moral living or church policy. He doesn't ask her to relocate, realign or reevaluate her rules. He declares her forgiven without baptism, communion or membership. It's just too much! By now Simon is convinced that this Yeshua is a radical who will have to be dealt with. In Simon's view, forgiveness *requires* right behavior. To offer forgiveness without expectation makes grace *cheap* and that will never do. Twenty centuries later, we are not so different. Yeshua looks on the total change of heart that results from God's divinely initiated act. He does not offer a checklist formula of grace to replace the checklist formula of sin. But we still demand conditions.

Why can Yeshua forgive with reckless abandon? Because He takes the cost of forgiveness on himself. He pays the price. If I sent you to Sak's and told you that I would pay for anything and everything you wanted, would you shop according to the rules or would you spend with reckless abandon? Yeshua can forgive without

---

[5] My debt for this wonderful insight is to Jonathan Winningham, pastor of Montverde Baptist Church

conditions because the debt I incurred is one that he will pay. Do we forgive in the same way? Is our forgiveness reckless because it comes from our willingness to embrace the cost? Or are we still trying to put some of the responsibility on the "forgiven" one?

There is something else. Forgiveness is not the end of the story. Forgiveness is the beginning.

"Go in peace." The Greek verb means a present and permanent state of fellowship with God. Forgiveness brings peace. Peace is the natural state of redeemed living. Not stress or guilt or shame or work or anxiety. Peace. Inner and outer harmony with God and creation. *Shalom* expresses well-being. Live life in harmony with yourself and your Creator. Have purpose. Enjoy significance. Discover the design of being alive.

Melanie and the woman in Simon's house both knew what it meant to find peace for troubled souls. They wept at His feet and joyful repentance for deliverance from lives of shame. Have you shed tears for sorrow and joy? Have you offered yourself as the towel of submission? Have you kissed His feet in love?

Have you heard Him say, "Daughter, go in *peace*"?

LOSS

How can I go on?

"Blessed are those who mourn" taught Yeshua. But anyone who knows the heartache of the loss this word implies must wonder where the blessing is. It is a funeral word, a word about death; not a word about remorse over past sins. A child dies. A husband dies. A friend dies. Where is the blessing when we stand at the grave site? Where is the comfort when we pack up the toys or the love letters or the photos? "Blessed" doesn't seem to be the right word at all when the tears will not stop, when the empty place in the heart will not be soothed.

Most of our experiences with this kind of loss are a mixture of unanticipated trauma and irreconcilable grief. Most of the time we are caught off guard. A car crash. A heart attack. An accident. Suddenly our world is torn, blood and tears bringing us to our knees, remembering what we should have said, what we could have done. But what would it be like to *know* that your greatest love was going to be taken from you and to helplessly watch it happen? What would you do if all the premonitions told you that the end was right around the corner and you could not stop it? What act would suffice to demonstrate your devotion, your commitment, your brokenness?

One woman will be remembered forever in a setting just like this. One woman's actions leave a legacy for every one of us who helplessly face unspeakable loss. Her encounter with Yeshua opens the way for all of us, the way to "blessed are those who mourn."

The story of John 12:1-9

"Yeshua therefore said, "Let her alone, in order that she may keep it for the day of My burial." John 12:7

Just a few days ago, the house was filled with unspeakable joy. It still seemed like a dream, but Lazarus sat at the table, breathing, eating, talking. Living proof that the grave could not hold him. Mary felt her heart beat a little louder. How foolish she had been when Yeshua arrived. Her face flush with the thought. She would never forget the words spoken to her sister: "I am the resurrection and the life." There was her brother, right before her eyes, as though nothing had happened. From grief to amazing joy in a few minutes. If only she could have those days back, even the sorrowful ones. How much better it would be than what she was feeling now.

The men seemed unaware of the background mood in the room. They spoke of the Passover. She heard a few quick remarks about the threats and the risk. But most of them had newfound confidence. How could anything happen to a man who could raise the dead? They felt invulnerable.

Mary saw something else. She saw the eyes of her Lord. They were distant now. Darkening. As if he were moving further and further away from them even as he shared the bread. He was really not part of the conversation. The voices bantered around him but he did not engage the others. Mary put her hand to her throat. It was shaking. She knew something terrible was coming. She could feel it.

Every woman encounters that moment in life when she knows someone deeply loved is gone. A parent whose fight with cancer ends. A husband who collapses on the job. A child who innocently steps into the street. A friend who is just driving to the store. Today it is usually a phone call. Or a knock on the door by a man in uniform. It is that crystalline moment when the world suddenly stops, frozen in time. Death's icy fingers grip your heart so painfully that doubt is squeezed from the equation. You just know. Before the words are even spoken. Before the tears. Before the gasps. You just know.

Mary watched her brother die. Just days before, she saw life flicker in his eyes as the illness consumed his body. She saw his eyes search for hers. She witnessed the moment of calm when there was nothing more to do but watch the light go out. She remembered the flame of hope; hope that Yeshua would come in time, burning, burning, glowing and then nothing but ash. But Yeshua did come. Where there was only ash, life appeared.

Now the hopeless feeling was back, stronger than ever. She knew. She felt the grip again. The cold. The vise constricting her breathing. But this time it was not her brother. It was her Master.

John's Gospel recounts this story with succinct poignancy. Martha is busy serving. Lazarus is busy eating. The disciples are busy talking. Only two people in the room are still and quiet. Only two know.

Mary took a pound of very expensive perfumed oil. She approached Yeshua. With quivering hands, she broke open the vase containing the mixture. Until that moment, no one paid much attention. The aroma gushed into the room with such power that everyone immediately turned toward her. But she saw only Yeshua. And in his eyes she saw his open acceptance of her gift.

Mark's account of this story (in 14:3-9) says that the woman poured the costly perfume first over his head. This act was an acknowledgement of royalty. David, Hazael, Solomon and others were declared God's chosen kings in this way. Perhaps the disciples saw the symbolism. They would like to have Yeshua rise as the new king, leading them to victory. But Mary, so close to her beloved rabbi, may have seen a deeper meaning. Anointing was also a sign of sanctification and consecration; an act performed by the priests before the sacrifice. Exodus tells us that Aaron was anointed as the high priest of the people, a role that Yeshua would play for all humanity. The laws governing sacrifices and the holy altar are replete with anointing. There is more than royalty. Certainly all these images are in mind here. Yeshua is the priest-king who will be sacrificed. It is an anointing of death. Mary anticipated what Yeshua already knew.

Let Mary transport you to the funeral preparation of your Lord. There is a dark side to the cross. It is the time when we connect with the cost of His sacrifice. What I most hoped to keep will be swallowed up in loss. Baptism is our identification with Yeshua in the tomb. It is the place where we join Him in sacrifice. Feel the oil, the perfume, the rhythms of the room. Unless you know the loss of the Master, you will never know the full joy of His return.

Yeshua died for me. In this moment before his death, Mary expresses the divine tragedy brought about by my human folly. Am I able to stand with her and weep over the part I played? Have I anointed my King into His death for me?

Loss (2)

"Yeshua therefore said, "Let her alone, in order that she may keep it for the day of My burial." John 12:7

John tells us that Mary knelt and anointed his feet. The heavy oil spilled onto her hands and through her fingers. With the care she would have given a new born, she spread the perfume over the rough skin. All those miles walking dusty roads. All those steps following the Father's will. Her hands cried out, "Oh, my Lord, is there no way for me to prevent just these next few steps?" But she knew she could not. She felt the cold.

Yeshua did not move when she let down her hair and began to wipe the perfume. The scent increased with the movement. She felt the salty taste of her tears, not realizing that she had been crying. The curtain of her long black hair removed everything from view except his feet. She let the tears flow freely.

Perhaps Mary is the *woman* of sorrows, acquainted with grief. Two men in her life treated her with respect, kindness, dignity and love. One died last week – and will die again. Now she senses that the other will also be taken from her. And there is nothing she can do but prepare for the funeral.

There are no parallels for anointing feet in any other first century literature. The action Mary took was unique. Anointing Yeshua's feet is an act of utter devotion and submission. Mary took perfume worth a year's wages and transformed it into a love offering without price. In the performance of a duty delegated to the lowest servants, Mary elevated the simplest of tasks to divinely inspired humility. Her tender care broke the boundaries of social protocol, gender intimacy and religious ritual. Why would she do such a thing? Because she loved him. That love connected her to the real meaning of this occasion. She honored the one thing that mattered most to her – Yeshua her Lord. Mary moved beyond the restraints of her culture in order to fulfill her one desire – to show him her devotion.

Both John and Mark tell us that the disciples, especially Judas, complained at the waste of this sacrifice. Their motives, selfish or not, were driven by calculation and comparison. They could not see what Mary saw. Blinded by their own agendas, their vacant eyes saw nothing but waste. The real disciple had eyes open to God. She prepared the body of her Lord for his death.

A woman who knows the sorrow of this kind of loss is immune to the criticism of uncomprehending observers. That criticism may be like the words of Judas ("What a waste. This should have been given to the poor") or it may be more like the criticism we might hear today ("She should get on with her life. There is nothing more she can do"). It really doesn't matter what insensitive clichés are bantered about. The intention is the same – to minimize the quality and depth of the love expressed. Underlying all these remarks is something more profound. Jealousy. A special kind of jealousy that says, "Why don't I feel like she does? What's the matter with me? Her expression is so unrestrained. Why can't I feel like that?" If I can't express such passionate devotion, I'll minimize it or deflect it. I'll knock her down a few rungs. I'll make sure she is no better than me.

But a woman of sorrows, acquainted with grief, knows that there is no substitute and no inoculation for devotion's broken heart. The gift of love knows nothing of waste.

Yeshua does not speak to Mary. He addresses his remark to those whose lives are filled with other agendas. He does not need to speak to her. She already understands. She has already given up her own conditions. She has already disarmed herself. She has already put herself in the place of complete surrender. She does not even need to be told that what she does is the most acceptable mixture of sacrifice and devotion God could ask. Mary prepares the Son for His greatest hour. God chose a woman of special character to bring about the entrance of His Son into the world. He chose a woman of equally special character to bring about His exit from the world. It is not a matter of religious duty or gender or personality. It is a matter of humility! These women were truly servants of the Lord. They understood their roles with a depth lost on their male counterparts. And they were not deterred from performing the tasks before them.

"Leave her alone." A rebuke and an affirmation in the same voice. Yeshua accepted Mary's offering and at the same time dismissed the disciples petty concerns. One sees, the others are blind. God's grace falls on the one who sees. Mark tells us that Yeshua specifically says Mary's act of submission and sacrifice is a good thing. John includes the deeper meaning. She is preparing him for burial.

The Greek word used in Yeshua' rebuke is *aphiemi*. It has several different meanings, all associated with the idea of letting go. It can mean "to dismiss, to give up, to let escape, to quit, to forsake, to let pass or to permit." Mary is not likely to have forgotten this word. It is the same word that Yeshua used when her brother stepped out of the tomb. "Unbind him and *let him go*." It is the word of power over death. But that is not all. There is another reason that Mary will have remembered this word. It is also the word for God's decision to *let go* of our sin. It is the word used for *forgiveness*. It is the word of power over guilt.

Yeshua reminds the audience that Mary knows both of these senses of *aphiemi* intimately. She has seen the power of unbinding death, and she knows that power of unloosing sins. Do not interfere with her, says Yeshua. She knows the intimate connection between death and sin, and she knows that I have power over both. "I am the resurrection and the life," he said to her. And she believes.

"You are my Lord, my Master and the one I live for," says Mary with her hands.

"She has kept this oil for the day of my burial." That day has arrived.

Every woman of sorrow and grief can prepare her loved one for the day of burial. With humility and devotion, every woman can fulfill the role that God has given her, anointing the one lost as a sacrifice consecrated to God. And every woman can hear the words echoed across the centuries, "Let it go. Let go of the cords of death. Let go of the guilt of sin. Let go of yourself and kneel at My feet. I am the resurrection and the life."

THANKLESSNESS

Does anyone treasure me?

Until the clamor of the feminist movement, women were perhaps the most unappreciated human beings on earth. Of course, feminism has not really solved the problem. Demanding equality does not guarantee genuine appreciation. Real appreciation must come from the heart, not the legislature. So women carry the burdens of society much of the time without honor or respect. And sometimes that weight just gets to be too much. This is the case with the story of Mary and Martha. Yeshua understood all the emotions and all of the relationships involved in feeling unrecognized. This story isn't just about women, but, of course, it certainly belongs among them – the unappreciated of the earth.

"but only a few things are necessary, really only one; for Mary has chosen the good part, which shall not be taken away from her." Luke 10:42

Martha will forever be remembered as the one who missed the point. Mary chose to hear the teaching of Yeshua. Martha chose to concern herself with being a good hostess. John's gospel says that Yeshua corrected her. We read these words and congratulate ourselves that we are like Mary. We know what is most important. We acknowledge that the words of Yeshua are God's words about life. Of course learning from Yeshua is more important than setting the table. Who could ever think otherwise?

But there are several tiny secrets hidden in this story that reveal another direction to Yeshua' thought. It's all in the verbs.

The story begins in Luke 10:38. The first thing we notice is that it is Martha who initiates the encounter. She asks Yeshua to her home. The verb is *hupodechomai*. It is often translated "receive" or "invite" or "welcome" but these translations cause us to miss something.

My wife is Sicilian. Her mother is Sicilian. Her father is Sicilian. From the moment you enter the home of my in-laws, you know you are welcomed. There are hugs and kisses and affection. They are glad to see you and they are not afraid to show it. Forget the limp handshakes and the innocuous "How have you been?" questions. If you aren't Italian (we can't all be that lucky), then go see *My Big Fat Greek Wedding*. You'll get the idea. It's family time. *You* are important.

Martha's action is the same expression of openhearted acceptance. The verb combines the thought of eager acceptance and underlying support. Martha said, "I can't wait to have you come to my house. You are so important to me. Please honor me with your presence." She opened her arms and her heart. How could Yeshua refuse? Martha's excitement and enthusiasm set the stage.

Then we see another picture. The second verb describes Mary's action. It is *parakathezomai*, a word that means to sit beside someone. Luke says that Mary sat down near the feet of Yeshua. Mary is not bustling with excitement over the arrival of a special guest. Mary chooses a different expression of welcome – being in the presence of a teacher. Mary's posture is the posture of the pupil. And, as we shall soon see, a bit more.

Sometimes when we visit my in-laws, their home is crowded with people. There are often many extra place settings at the table. After dinner if we sit together and talk, more likely than not there is not enough space on the sofa. So, I like to sit on the floor, right next to my wife so that I feel her feet and legs. It is comforting. It says, "I love you and don't want to be away from your presence, even if it means a less comfortable spot". It's nice to feel so close to her.

Mary chose closeness over welcoming hugs. That left Martha with the preparation tasks, and that's the focus of this story.

Our third verb is translated "distracted." It is *periespato*. It paints an interesting picture. It is all about breathing. The root word, *spao*, is the word "to pull, to draw out and to breathe." But when we add the prefix *peri* we get the sense of being pulled or drawn out in all different directions at the same time. It is trying to breathe in and out all at once. Do you know what happens when you do that? You choke. Breathing is all about rhythm and flow. *Periespato* is about choking and gasping. The natural flow is disturbed.

One of my friends is Dr. Ben Lerner, author of the best-selling book, *Body By God*. Ben makes an interesting observation about life. If you do not *schedule* your time, you will find that you have no time to schedule. It's a matter of priorities. Ben tries to help us see that if we want a deeper spiritual encounter with Yeshua, we have to make appointments with Him. If we want a healthier body, we have to schedule exercise. If we want better relationships with the ones we love, we have to plan time with them. The pressures of this world, the pace of this life and the constant confusing bombardment of unimportant but necessary demands will drain away all of your time unless you have unbreakable commitments to a schedule. It is the double yellow line theory of living. Paint double yellow lines around those things that really matter. Then DO NOT CROSS over them. They are sacred times, set aside for special purposes. God made the Sabbath sacred. The rest is up to us.

We all agree with Yeshua – Mary made the right choice. But I suspect that we all live much more like Martha.

I know I should spend time in the morning reading my Bible and listening to God, but.
I want to pray more, but.
I know I need to spend time with ones who are suffering, but.
I wish I could take a few minutes to meditate on His word, but.
I really want to get together with Christian friends, but.
I need to attend the weekly small group study, but.
I know my spouse and I need time just together, but.

The "but" list is long.

But: The kids have practice.
      The car needs gas.
      The laundry isn't done.
      The conference call was long.
      The hairdresser took forever.
      The reports had to be done again.
      The refrigerator was empty.
      The dog got sick.
      The bills were due.
      The gym was crowded.

You can easily add more to the "but" list. Martha is trying. Lord knows she is trying. She is trying to keep all the balls in the air at the same time. She is trying to meet all of the expectations at once. She is trying to breathe in and out at the same time. She is trying to be the First Century Supermom.

Martha knew what was needed to make her guest feel at home. She poured herself into the tasks with one goal in mind – to please Yeshua.   She was the one who welcomed the Lord.   Now she wanted everything to be "just perfect". But something happened in her zeal to make everything right. There was a shift in attitude.

Thanklessness (2)

"but only a few things are necessary, really only one; for Mary has chosen the good part, which shall not be taken away from her."
Luke 10:42

Martha had a lot on her mind. A dinner party means attending to plenty of details. But in her desire to please her guest, she encountered more than culinary complications.

Luke tells us that all of the distractions about serving altered her attitude. This thought hides a deeper reality. The word Luke uses for "serving" is *diakonian*. It is part of the word family of *diakonos*. This is the basis of our word "deacon." In the New Testament, Yeshua uses this word when he says, "whoever wishes to become great among you shall be your servant" (Matthew 20:26). To be a servant of others is a mark of adopting the vision of Yeshua. Yeshua's leadership was servant leadership. It is not Martha's anxiousness to serve that is the problem. She is behaving in a way that we would probably applaud. She is working behind the scenes on behalf of others. She is carrying the load so that others may benefit. But Yeshua never looks for outward action as the sign of a servant. Outward humility can disguise inner pride. And this is Martha's problem.

"She came up to Yeshua," says Luke. Body language often tells a lot more than words. Luke uses the verb *ephistemi*. This word combines the prefix for "near" (*epi*) and the verb "to stand" (*histemi*). We need to see the picture clearly. Mary is *sitting* at the feet of Yeshua, listening to Him speak. Martha comes to Yeshua, but she does not sit. She does not kneel. She does not bend. She *stands* near him. In all likelihood, she stands *over* him since he was probably not standing while he talked. She takes the

Jesus Said To Her

posture of confrontation. She demands attention. We know exactly how this feels. It is that moment when someone outside the conversation inserts a presence that demands attention. Whatever Yeshua was teaching had to stop because Martha pushed her presence into the room. She made a stand.

It takes only a moment to blurt out her indignation. The behavior of a servant cannot restrain the spirit of the slighted. She exhibits an attitude that demands personal rights.

"Lord, do you not care that my sister has left me to do all the serving alone? Then tell her to help me."

How many times have we said that same thing? Yeshua, don't you care that I have to do this all by myself? Yeshua, why can't you send someone to help me? Yeshua, if you really loved me, why don't you lift this burden from me? As the Beatles so clearly put it – "I, me, me, mine." Martha's interest in serving is not from the devotion of unacknowledged submission. She wants life to be fair. Why do I have to do everything myself? The ultimate question of pride. I should be in charge of life so that things would be fair (for me). And by the way, if you think this is only a problem for women, you need to remember Yeshua's *final* remark to Peter (John 21:22). Martha gets to learn the lesson now. Peter had to learn the lesson after the resurrection.[6]

"Do you not care?" The words tell us more than first appears. Martha uses the Greek word *ou* for "not." This is a strong negative. It means "never" and opposed to "not according to circumstances." "You never cared about me." "You never think about what I need." "You never bother to ask what I want." Have

---

[6] For an examination of Peter's lesson, see my article, *God Isn't Fair*, on my web site skipmoen.com

those words ever come from your mouth? Then you know the expression of Martha. "Yeshua, you never cared."

In Greek, the verb translated "care" covers a range from "give forethought and concern" to "care and interest for someone." This word reveals part of Martha's real character. This is a "get attention" word. "No one is paying any attention to me," says Martha. "I am doing all the work but I am being ignored." Life isn't fair when no one seems to show interest in my problems.

We need to take a personal inventory here. Martha is performing "good" service. She is doing what needs to be done in order to accommodate Yeshua. She is busy on behalf of the Lord. But it is *her* idea of service, not *His*. She isn't doing anything wrong, she just has the wrong goal. Her motive is to serve, but her goal was to serve *her way*. And as a result, she feels unrecognized for her efforts. Does this sound a little like you and me?

Martha wants more than recognition. She wants someone to accommodate her needs. She thinks to herself, "I am not getting the recognition and help I deserve. Someone is to blame." And the first person on the blame list is God.

Martha does not confront Mary. Martha uses the triangle approach, combined with a strong dose of guilt. What Martha claims she wants is Mary's help. As we shall see, this is only the surface. To get what she wants, she plays two games – guilt and blame. "If you really cared about me, you would do . . . ." The first shot fired is guilt. "Don't you see that I am important? Don't you see that I am burdened? Don't you know how hard I am working for you, Lord?" Feel guilty that you have not done anything to help me. Respond to me because you are responsible and you have failed to meet my expectations.

Martha goes to the authority figure. Clearly Mary's action shows she is ready to do whatever Yeshua says, so Martha attempts to enlist Yeshua in her effort to get Mary to meet her need. Martha uses a third party to play the guilt game. She wants Yeshua to feel guilty that He has not recognized her need and therefore instruct Mary to act accordingly. But Martha is not finished.

The second shot is blame. "My sister has left me." The Greek word translated "left" is *kataleipo*. This verb is an *intensified* form of a word that means "to forsake or to leave behind." Martha is not making casual conversation here. She is not suggesting that Mary has accidentally overlooked the kitchen duties. Martha complains that she has been *abandoned* to the servant tasks. Mary has forsaken her, left her hanging and deliberately put all the problems on her shoulders while she spends (wastes?) her time listening to Yeshua. And, oh yes, there is another side issue here. Women in First Century Judaism were forbidden instruction by a Rabbi. Martha may also have been jealous that Yeshua tacitly approved of Mary's breech of social protocol (although we know that Yeshua also taught Martha). But the combination of factors clearly leads Martha to voice her real attitude – "I should be recognized and put in charge."

Do you find the tactics familiar? Engage another in the confrontation, supply guilt, add blame and solicit sympathy and action. For one purpose – meet my need.

We are often like Martha. We exhibit the behaviors of being a servant. Outwardly we appear to embrace Yeshua's directive. But we lack the motive of unacknowledged sacrifice. We want recognition for our efforts. We want others to say, "Oh, what a marvelous job you're doing. You are so humble and gracious."

When we don't get personal accolades for our tasks, injustice raises its head. We spread guilt like butter. We pour out the blame while we pour the water. We forget that sacrificial service is done for the audience of One.

God never suggests that serving in His name will result in recognition. In fact, if we accept Yeshua's insight and example, we should expect to be overlooked, ignored and even ridiculed for taking the role of the servant. But it is God's way. Serving Him by serving others is not aimed at personal acknowledgement.

Many times as I write about the depths of God's word, I find myself saying, "All those people that I send this to just don't seem to care. Why don't they write to me telling me how much it means to them? Why don't the publishers give me praises about my penetrating thoughts? Here I am all alone, fighting this battle for you God, and no one seems to care." I have the Martha complex. Fortunately I have an insightful wife who gently reminds me, "Who are you really trying to serve – the readers or God?"

That is the first lesson of Martha. When it comes to serving God, audience is everything. And in His line of serving, the only audience is the audience of One. Are you in the kitchen being busy so that you will be recognized by all the guests, or are you serving only One?

Thanklessness (3)

"but only a few things are necessary, really only one; for Mary has chosen the good part, which shall not be taken away from her." Luke 10:42

Oswald Chambers' devotional for February 13 suggests that there is a devotion of hearing that comes when we are close to Yeshua. The destiny of my development with God is to be so in touch with Him that I hear Him speaking to me as a *routine* part of my daily life. Mary is learning this aspect of devotion. But Martha stopped listening when she decided to make her stand. She heard her own voice demanding recognition rather than the voice of Yeshua teaching humility.

Yeshua answers Martha. "Martha, Martha." The repetition of her name is not an indictment or exasperation. It is an indication of tenderness. Today we would say, "Oh, Martha," as we reach out and put an arm around her shoulders.

"You are anxious." Yeshua uses a powerful word for "anxious". It is the same word he uses in Matthew 6 when he says, "*So do not **worry** about tomorrow, for tomorrow will take care of itself.*"

The Greek word is from the verb *merimnao*. It means anxiety that disrupts the tranquil state of mind and disturbs the personality. This is not a word about being careful or cautious. It is a word about an emotional state that is preoccupied with concern. It is life when we just can't stop thinking about the problems. It's that mental state when something bothers us so much that we just can't get past it.

Yeshua adds one other description to his assessment of Martha's state of mind. He says, "You are troubled." The word is *turbaze*.

Think of the seething movement of a large, noisy crowd. Pushing and shoving, yelling and arguing. Have you ever been caught in a crowd like that? Just trying to stay on your feet is difficult. Getting to the edge of the tumult is nearly impossible. You are pushed along with the mass no matter where it goes. Yeshua says to Martha, "Your inner thoughts are like that unruly crowd. They are pushing you along, out of control. Your emotional anxiety and inner tumult have caused you to make this stand. But it is not the role of the servant."

Yeshua redirects her. If we are not careful, we might think Yeshua is pointing from "many" to "one." But Martha's issue is not "many things." Yeshua is not teaching about setting priorities. He is not suggesting that life should be lived in quiet contemplation. It is equally possible to be anxious and troubled over one thing. Yeshua does not focus on *quantity*. He reveals something else. He looks at the motivation and attitude of his follower, Martha. He sees her filled with personal striving and emotional turmoil. Her devotion has been diverted to her own goals.

Our text reads, *"but only a few things are necessary,* **really only one**:*"* This English translation seems to place the emphasis on the *number* of items we manage. But the Greek says, "but one is needed." Yeshua has focused on what is essential; what is needed. The phrase is *henos esti chreia* (one is necessary). *Chreia* is a word of *personal need.* It conveys the idea of something required to fulfill a debt, a personal necessity. Yeshua sees that Martha is asking for something quite personal – recognition. But Yeshua knows that what Martha believes to be her need is not her real necessity. She does not need the temporary recognition that she demands (acknowledge my efforts and provide me with help). The need to be filled in her life must come through a much deeper recognition of the servant character of God.

For Martha, this is a defining moment. Life is designed to bring us into the circumstances of our defining moment – the moment when who we really are in the depths of our being shines forth. The problem with "defining moments" is this: you never know when they are going to arrive. A defining moment is not like an exam in school or a professional license test or an interview for a promotion. A defining moment is that sudden crossroads of circumstances that reveals a lifetime of character. You can't cram for it. It's not about what you know. It's about who you are.

Think back over your years on this planet. What were your defining moments? What were the circumstances that suddenly revealed your real character? They were probably times when you were off guard, times when you reacted according to your true instincts rather than the carefully scripted behaviors. Unfortunately, some of those moments we would rather not think about. And that's exactly what happened to Martha.

This is the last sentence of the Mary-Martha story, the sentence that forever defined Martha as the one who was preoccupied with tasks but missed the important thing. She was so busy with all the clutter of life that she overlooked what was essential. It is a defining moment that haunts her – a moment that is remembered through history.

Yeshua wants Martha to know that there is one critical need to be filled in her life. Yeshua does not say that Martha's actions aren't important. He doesn't dismiss her attempts to please him. He simply says that her anxiety about "doing everything right" has caused her to be blind to the one critical element of this defining moment – the element of servant devotion. Martha allows the pressures of life to alter her deepest character. She makes room for frustration and complaint when all she really needed to do was focus on devotion to her Lord. Life is not about what she does. It is about who she is.

The defining moment will usually be the intersection of pressure and priority, that split second when you will choose frustration or devotion. It's a matter of character, not performance.

The story isn't finished until we see the contrast that Yeshua emphasizes. Mary has *chosen* the good part. The verb is *eklego*. In the New Testament, the verb always involves *personal* preference between many choices. It is not the choice between good and bad. It is the choice between what I prefer and what I do not like. Would you rather have that in yellow or blue? Do you prefer strawberries or raspberries?

What has Mary selected? She has selected the "good part." Here the words convey the idea of what is useful, beneficial and profitable. She has shown her preference for what is most valuable to her. She has selected the part that meets her deepest *personal* need. But you, Martha, have not selected what would have met your *personal* need. Instead, you tried to substitute action for attitude. This defining moment reveals what you lack.

Is Yeshua commending Mary's choice but rejecting Martha's? Many commentators suggest the passage teaches that the highest form of service is found in devotion and fellowship. Devotion to Yeshua is surely the "good part." But the verb of "choice" is not a verb of *exclusion*. It is a verb of preference. Perhaps Yeshua is not teaching a higher pathway of spiritual enlightenment so much as he is meeting the real need of the "distracted" woman. This is a story about the need for recognition and the source of that recognition. Every woman will discover that life is cluttered with distractions. But the woman of God will realize that the call of the servant is not based on personal acknowledgement by others. It is based on the acknowledgement of the audience of One. Just like Martha, we will feel abandoned until we see that our deepest need for recognition is found in choosing His way.

GRIEF

Who will care for me now?

"There's nothing left in life for me. I just can't go on." When we reach this point, we need more than an encouraging word or a supportive hug. We need to be rescued. We need someone to sweep onto the scene and *fix* things. A few noble sentiments or an uplifting speech just won't cut it. Life at the edge needs real action. Fortunately, Yeshua is the God who acts. He knows our deepest needs and He knows when we are on the precipice. Paul tells us that God will not allow us to be tempted with more than we can handle, but sometimes it seems as though God's view of my capacity is just a bit more than my view. Certainly women know what it means to run on empty. But even they come to the end. In this amazing story from Luke, we discover that Yeshua knows more about grief than we thought, and He is willing to act on our behalf. This is a story for every women who has come to the edge of the cliff and peered into the abyss – and then discovered the restraining hand of the Savior, calling her back to life among the living.

"He felt compassion for her, and said to her, "Do not weep." Luke 7:13

Nain. The village named "pleasant" or "beautiful". But on this day the Hebrew name does not fit the mood at all. Today is the day of a funeral. Today is a mother's worst nightmare – death invades life. Her only son is carried to the grave.

Luke tells us that the day after Yeshua healed the slave of the Centurion, he traveled to this village. A large crowd accompanied him. And why not? They were anxious to be in the presence of such a great miracle worker. Even a Centurion recognized Yeshua's reputation as a powerful man of God. The crowd could not have been more enthralled.

As Yeshua approaches the city gate, he comes upon a scene of grief. The funeral procession moves through the gate, carrying the body of a man. Within minutes the crowd discovers that this man is the only son of a poor widow. Many of the townspeople are walking with her, attempting to console her while they lament the cruel hand of God. To lose a husband is difficult enough. But to lose an only son after losing a husband. What will she do now? She has no one to care for her. The fate of widows and orphans was well known. She looked forward to poverty and abandonment.

There are two critical words in this very brief encounter. The first describes Yeshua's character; the second his action. They are inseparable.

"And when the Lord saw her, He felt compassion for her." Compassion. The Greek word is *splanchnizomai*. It is the original Greek word for "intestines." Over time the word became associated with those emotions that deeply upset us. In particular, it is connected with pity. This word is very graphic and very physical.

Imagine those times in your life when something affected you so dramatically that it literally "turned your stomach." You had a hot flash. You felt faint. What you saw brought instant discomfort, an outrage at life's inequity. It is the immediate reaction over something tragic. Everyone in America got a taste of this on September 11. A nation's heartache and agony.

We keep ourselves at a comfortable distance from this feeling. It is just too hard to deal with. But sometimes it catches us off guard and we break. I remember driving on a New Jersey freeway after an evening meeting. The radio announced that a man had boarded the train in Long Island and randomly began killing people. Nine were dead before he was stopped. The voice on the radio shattered me. I saw the bodies of fathers, mothers, children and the families left behind. I didn't know any of these people, but I began to cry, so much I had to stop driving. I could do nothing but pray. The bullets that ripped through those families hit me too. All of those lives wasted because of evil. Satan laughed at us. But I cried with Yeshua. This world was not supposed to be like this.

Yeshua and the disciples are walking toward Nain. They are probably busy talking among themselves about the past few days. Their thoughts are about the amazing miracle of healing. Of course, they didn't actually *see* the miracle. Yeshua never reached the Centurion's home. But the crowd was convinced. All the reports confirmed that the slave was well.

Suddenly they come upon the funeral. It was certainly not the first funeral the crowd witnessed. Death was a constant companion of those who lived in Roman occupied lands. But today it must have been a "cold shower" shock. Everyone was thinking about the slave who had just escaped death. Now the reality of the inevitable slapped them in the face. The crowd slipped from the mountaintop experience and suddenly tumbled into the Valley of the Shadow of Death. "Yesterday," sang Paul McCartney, "all my troubles seemed so far away. Now it looks as though they're here to stay." We all want to believe in yesterday.

It is the universal roller coaster of life. Slowly we climb to the top, feeling the thrill of finally getting over the hump. We relish the view. We breathe the clean air. The sun is warm. And then the car drops. We are screaming toward the bottom. Life is coming apart at the seams. It is chaos and terror. That moment on the top is forgotten in the acceleration toward destruction.

Yeshua stopped. The crowd jolted with him. Compassion. A rough, physical word expressing the jarring, disorienting feeling of life gone haywire. Everything wonderful about the view from the top ripped away by the serrated edge of death.

Splanchnon presents an unusual word mystery. Most Greek words have direct Hebrew associations. But *splanchnon* has no Hebrew connection. When we look for a Hebrew connection, we find a different Greek word – *oiktiro* – the word for "sympathy." *Splanchnon* is a word that surfaces much later. But by the time Luke related this story in Greek, *splanchnon* had taken over the meaning "pity" and "sympathy." That isn't the end of the this curious story. The Hebrew concept eventually captured by *splanchnon* helps us see an important distinction. The Hebrew word behind pity and sympathy is *racham*. But *racham* is the Hebrew word for "womb." In Hebrew thought it is the symbol of intense, personal identification. Nothing establishes a bond of identity more than the same birth mother. When emotions cause us to completely identify with our common humanity, with being born into this world, we experience *racham*. The unity of brothers and sisters, the bond of parents and children, is extended to evoke the shared experience of being one who is born – and one who dies. From God's point of view, we are all brothers and sisters. When *splanchnon* took over the meaning of this Hebrew concept, it carried with it the intense identification of common humanity, an identification that was particularly acute in times of trouble.

There is still more to this story. The Hebrew concept is not limited to a "feeling." Sympathy is an emotional response of heartfelt identification. Pity is an emotional response to another's suffering. Empathy is an emotional response to common-bond oneness. But *racham* is more than emotion. It is *action* elicited by emotion. *Racham* is the action of love expressed as a result of sympathy or pity. *Racham* does not pass by the circumstances of sorrow with a mournful sigh. *Racham* steps into life's heartbreaking trials and actively engages in an effort to lift the burden. Zechariah 7:9 instructs us to "make and accomplish compassion." Psalm 69:16 calls for the action of compassion from the God who is filled with compassionate acts. Divine compassion is not an arm around the shoulder and a shared tear. Compassion is warfare! It is active resistance to evil in a world that has come crashing down. Compassion is *me* taking the place of *you*. It is personal action identification. It is Yeshua on the cross, enduring brutality, horror and torture for my sake because *God is compassionate*.

The most common subject of the word *racham* is God Himself. From the Old Testament context, it is abundantly clear that compassion is not an action prompted by the merit of the suffering party. I don't earn compassion. God's compassion, and the compassion of all who follow His example, is relief given simply because it can be given. If I am to follow the model of Yeshua, my *actions of relief* will not be based on how worthy the suffering person is. My actions will be based only on my ability to offer help because I can without any thought of reciprocity.

Exodus 34:6 is God's self-definition. The very first word God uses to describe Himself is "compassionate." If you gave your own self-definition, would that be the first word on your lips? The widow of Nain provides us with a window into the heart of God – and what we find is *racham*. The God Who cares.

Grief (2)

"He felt compassion for her, and said to her, "Do not weep." Luke 7:13

Tragedy is the opportunity for the display of God's glory. Compassion is the active ingredient in that display.

Yeshua is the man of *racham*. He does not just *feel* the common bond of human life. He *acts*. He practices compassion. Other than Yeshua's parables, the Greek equivalent of *racham* is never used to describe any human being *except* Yeshua. *Splanchnon* is **the** word for the divine nature of Yeshua's acts. It is the active verb of the story of the Good Samaritan, the wicked servant and the prodigal son. It is a description of the very essence of God's compassion.

When Luke introduces Yeshua's response with *splanchnon*, the stage is set for action. Compassion means response. When Joseph finally came face to face with Benjamin after twenty years of separation, he was so moved that he had to rush from the room to weep privately. Emotion brings action. When Solomon commands the living child to be divided in half in order to determine justice, the mother immediately volunteers to give up the child rather than have it killed. Emotion brings action. Yeshua turns to the widow and says, "Do not weep." God's compassion is about to bring action.

Weeping is not strong enough to capture this emotion. The phrase is *me klaie*. It means, "Do not lament." *Klaio* is the verb that describes the physical display of grief. It is not just tears. Have you been to the funeral of a deeply loved one? This is devastating grief. It is that deep groan that cannot be consoled. Your heart has been torn in two and there is no surgeon who can repair the damage. It is beyond shedding tears. This is body-despair.

In Jewish thought, death was considered the final destiny of Man. The only consolation was a long and prosperous life. When someone died "before his time," Jewish theology usually attributed this tragedy to punishment for sins. An early death was God's way of expunging the blight of sin on the community. This widow not only suffered loss. She also suffered the stigma of punishment. Now her community would begin to wonder, "What did this young man do to deserve God's swift retribution? Or perhaps what did his mother do, since God has punished both the husband and the son?" The widow's grief is multiplied by her inevitable questionable status in Nain. She will live under the double curse – alone and suspect.

The Greek word *klaio* is associated with the Hebrew word *bakah*. This Hebrew verb also means, "to weep, cry out loud or lament," but there is an additional thought present in the Hebrew that is not necessarily found in the Greek. Since Luke is translating these events into Greek, we must understand the Hebrew mindset if we are to fully comprehend the circumstances. *Bakah* displays that same *outward* signs but the inner thought pattern is different. *Bakah* is lament to *God*. It is the expression of complete dependence on God as the giver of life. In fact, the entire nation can raise its prayer of lament to Him as an act of humble dependence. The widow in our story is not simply expressing outward human grief over her circumstances; she is at the same time raising her voice to God acknowledging her total dependence on Him.

Klaio is used only once of Yeshua, when he looked out over the city of Jerusalem and "wept" because the people would not come to the Father. Yeshua never wept (*klaio*) over death. When he confronts the tomb of Lazarus, the Greek text uses a different word with an entirely different meaning. Yeshua did not weep over death because death was not humanity's burden. Separation and rejection is humanity's burden. Separation and rejection cause real grief.

"Do not grieve," says Yeshua to this widow. God hears you. Death can be reversed. The temporary quality of death is even indicated in the choice of the word for "not." Here it is *me*, the "not" of present circumstance. This is the "not" that belongs to the existing conditions. It is only appropriate as long as the conditions prevail. It is the "not" of "I might not go with you" or "We do not carry that brand." There is another word for "not" in Greek (*ou*) which is closer to "never.". Yeshua tells this widow, "The conditions for your grief are about to change. Weeping is no longer appropriate. So stop." In essence, he says, "What looks like a permanent situation is only a temporary condition. Death is not (never) the end." In the face of what we all consider the finish line, Yeshua says, "No, we aren't done here." *Splanchnizomai* is about to turn *klaio* into rejoicing.

What useless comfort it would be for Yeshua to embrace this widow and say, "Life goes on, you know. Buck up. God will take care of your needs." How insensitive would it be for Yeshua to say, "I'm so sorry I couldn't be here for you. I was so busy with that Centurion thing, and, you know, I just couldn't come any sooner," or "I'll make sure that the church knows about your grief. We'll have a special prayer session with the elders." Perhaps Yeshua could have echoed the worst of our misguided sympathy, "God moves in mysterious ways. We can't understand now but it will all be for the best." None of these inane comments, no matter how well intended, will repair the damage this woman faces. She will still be alone and she will still live with the stigma of punishment. Yeshua provides a different solution.

Divine compassion is not heavenly sympathy. Yeshua acts. The Greek tells us that he came near to the coffin. We might consider such an act because today our coffins are antiseptically discrete, closed boxes that keep us just that necessary space away from the dead. But this was a bier, an open platform for transporting the dead to the place of internment. The body was undoubtedly wrapped for burial. Religious law strictly controlled the process. Dealing with the dead created serious problems with ritual defilement. Rabbinic law required the dead to be buried within the same day if possible. In the climate of the Near East, deterioration presented health issues. For Yeshua to come near the bier would already be strange. Avoiding contact was essential for both reasons. But what Yeshua did next would have caused everyone to gasp.

The Greek verb is *haptomai*. Translated "touch," it is really "handled with the intent of exerting influence." We should see this as "embraced" or "clutched" or "grasped." Luke tells us that the bearers stopped. We understand why as soon as we understand the verb. Yeshua interfered with their movement by handling the dead man's bier. Luke's description that the bearers stopped may be more from shock than from impeded movement. What Rabbi would ever reach up and handle a dead man's platform?

And He said, "Young man, I say to you, arise." Rise up! A command, but in the *passive*. Essentially it means, "Wake yourself up!" The underlying thought of this verb is to wake up from sleep. Now we see what Yeshua saw. The young man's death is nothing more than sleep. He needs to wake up. This is the same thought in Yeshua's mind when he speaks about Lazarus ("Our friend Lazarus has fallen asleep, but I go, that I may awaken him." John 11:11). Death, the ultimate tragedy in the human arena, is no more serious an issue than sleep when Yeshua turns attention to it. Yeshua's command is all that is required to restore wakefulness. In one second, Yeshua overturns all the rules about life and living. The widow's world, crushed in the accelerating rush toward destruction, is transformed. Not alone. Not judged. Restored in every way.

The dead man sat up and began speaking. Not re-animated. Restored. Fully functioning. Perfectly normal. Just like waking up from a nap.

Yeshua's last act is the most telling. Luke says that Yeshua "gave him back to his mother." It is a gift from God. Dependence on God brings response. God is the God who gives. The word for "gave" is *didomi*, a verb that means "to give by deliberate choice as an act of good will." The same verb describes God's act of good will in John 3:16. God gave. This verb has a secondary meaning of delivering over to someone's charge. Yeshua gives this son back into the charge of his mother as a deliberate act of favor.

When the Centurion's slave was healed, the crowd felt enthusiasm and rejoicing. But the Centurion's slave was not dead. He was still alive even though the illness would have killed him. The incident at Nain brings a completely different response. The people are afraid. It is one thing to see illness reversed. That kind of activity is within the realm of the possible. But to see a dead man rise pushes humanity to the edge of credibility. There is no explanation except God.

The widow of Nain opens a window on the character of God. God is connected to our human condition, not only by Creation but also by identification. God's great self-definition puts compassion first. *Then the LORD passed by in front of him and proclaimed, "The LORD, the LORD God, compassionate and gracious, slow to anger, and abounding in lovingkindness and truth;"* (Exodus 34:6). This widow's grief is a glimpse of the grief God feels over those separated from Him. His lament is the heavenly wailing over needless sorrow. God is our Mother too. If *racham* describes compassion, then it describes God's feelings toward us with a term that evokes pregnancy and birth. The bond could not be deeper. God is in the "birthing" business. He wants us to live again. The widow of Nain came face-to-face with God's compassion in action. So can we. Do you hear Yeshua saying to you, "Do not weep?"

MISSION

What should I do?

Don't we just want God to tell us what to do next? Don't we really want the Bible in GPS translation? "Turn right in 100 yards" becomes "Marry the girl in the blue dress standing by the fountain," or "Take the second job offer you get on Wednesday." Oh, and if you make a mistake by not paying attention, then God's voice from the GPS Bible says, "You missed my direction. I am recalibrating. Please choose the third church on the east side of Maple Lane to attend this Sunday."

How many times have we come to a crossroad with the Lord and realized that we don't have a map? "Which way shall I go, Father?" "What should I do now?" We look for the GPS Bible guide to life, but we soon discover that God isn't in the electronic manufacturing business. He is in the relationship-dependence business. There are no maps. There is only trust.

Why are we so intent on having God's GPS system for our lives? Part of the answer lies in the preoccupation we have with control and predictability. We want certainty in our lives. We want to know what's going to happen so that we can be fully prepared, control the circumstances and keep everything in order. Guess what? The world is broken. It just doesn't work that way. And even if it did, I'm not so sure that God would allow you to get away with such immaturity. The women who encountered Yeshua after the resurrection found that life

wasn't predictable, but it was surprisingly joyful. Maybe that's what we all need to learn.

The story of Matthew 28:1-10

"Then Yeshua said to them, 'Do not be afraid; go and take word to My brethren to leave for Galilee, and there they shall see Me.'" Matthew 28:10

"Oh, God, how could this happen?" the women thought as they walked toward the tomb. Yeshua has been crucified. All of his disciples are in hiding. Why? Because they are afraid for their own lives. They won't even venture to the burial site. What if the Romans and the Sadducees are still looking for them? "I just don't care," Mary said to herself. "I have to go once more. Just to be near him."

On the first morning after the Sabbath, we find women going to offer a memorial. The disciples probably thought, "Well, we won't stop them. After all, they've never crucified a woman. So they will probably be okay. But we'll just wait here, where it's safe."

What happened to all that bravado before the arrest? Gone. What happened to the bickering over who would be second in command? Forgotten. What happened to the thrill of empowerment? Evaporated. The disciples were a wonderful testimony to all of those years of explanation and coaching. When things looked bad, they all ran away. If it sounds familiar, it should. We often act out the John Wayne version of true grit – good only while the camera is rolling.

It is no accident that women were the first to see the risen Lord. They were attending to the duties of life, just as women always have. Preparing meals, caring for children, cleaning, shopping, managing the domestic burdens. And, of course, taking care of the

Jesus Said To Her

sick and bringing flowers to the graves. These are roles men consider too menial for them. After all, men are the ones in authority (at least they like to think they are). The everyday issues of living should be delegated to others. So these women come to the tomb, ready to perform one more of the tasks that befall those who serve. As we soon discover, the act of serving brings us into close proximity with the glory of God.

Why are women the first see the resurrected Messiah? Perhaps we are too quick to ascribe this action to culture alone. While it is true that women took care of the daily tasks of families, perhaps there is a deeper reason behind the engineering of events to bring women to the tomb first. Cheryl Durham[7] suggests the answer may be related to women as nurturers by design. In this capacity, women come into closer proximity with God because their senses are attuned to noticing nuances of relational aspects. They experience care from the heart. This sensitivity seems to be part of God's original design. After all, He *built* the woman as *'ezer kenegdo* (inadequately translated as "helper").[8]

Two women came to show respect. Two women whose lives were filled with devotion for Yeshua. Two women who had never been the same since the day they met him. They came to grieve. They came to absorb once more the thoughts and feelings of this man. They came because they were still followers. Death did not destroy their commitment.

We all know the story. They encounter an angel who pronounces the good news. They are overwhelmed with fear and rejoicing. Can it be true? It was almost too much to hope. As the run back toward the city, Yeshua meets them.

---

[7] in private correspondence

[8] For a full discussion of the divinely ordained role of the *'ezer kenegdo*, please listen to *The Role of the 'ezer* at skipmoen.com/products

Matthew says that he stopped them with a greeting. The word Matthew uses is *chairete*. Rejoice! Joy to you! Immediately something has changed. This is not the word we expect. Except for the deceptive greeting of Judas and the mocking homage of the Roman soldiers, this word is used for much more than a common greeting. We find it on the lips of Yeshua and in the letters of Paul as an exclamation pregnant with the power of God's restoration. It is never found in the Old Testament as a greeting. The common Hebrew greeting should have been *shalom* – peace! *Shalom* in its true context means completeness, wholeness, harmony or fulfillment in both our undertakings and our relationships. This kind of peace is the result of God's promise. This was the common greeting of every Jew – a wish of God's well being for another. But *shalom* no longer fits reality.

Today that wish for well-being has been fulfilled. *Shalom*, the hope of peace, has become *chairete* – the announcement of grace. Yeshua proclaims a shift in the entire universe with one of life's simple tasks – greeting another. For thousands of years, mankind waited, expressing the wish for peace. On this day, peace has arrived, never to be taken away. Yeshua transforms the simplest of human interactions into a divine intersection. A meal becomes a sacrifice. A touch becomes a window on God's character. A greeting becomes the proclamation of fulfillment.

The four gospels do not report the same stories about the events at the tomb. They each have a different perspective and a different purpose. Matthew tells us that these women immediately fell to his feet and worshipped him. Actually, Matthew is a bit more explicit. He says that they *seized* his feet. The word is *ekratesan* from the verb *krateo*. They grabbed on and held fast. The root behind this word is the idea of strength. They were not about to let him go, ever again.

We need to feel the adrenaline rush of wonder *and* panic in this word. One of these women had only days before anointed these same feet with costly perfumed oil. She knew that she was preparing him for death. She never thought she would hold his feet again. With tears and her own hair, she wiped the scent of death from him. And now, somehow, he stood before her. Alive! She lost him once; she would not lose him again. So she *seized* his feet. "You must stay with me. You cannot go. I will not let you go. Not again."

Both women worshipped him. The word includes the idea of falling prostrate before him as a visible sign of obeisance. Literally, it means, "to throw a kiss" as a sign of respect and honor. Once again the past is revisited. Anointed feet kissed from a heart of incredible devotion. Washed by tears of repentance and joy. The Savior of their souls was saved. Suddenly they realized that this special man was much more than they could have imagined. "Lord, I worship you."

Before the risen Christ empowers these women with a message that would revolutionize the entire world, he allows them to display their relief, joy, wonder and commitment. He is patient with all of us, waiting until we are ready to seize his feet and never let him go, waiting until we fall before him in honor and reverence. The first step toward a mission is not a step toward those who need to hear what we have to say. It is a step toward the one who commissions us. It is the step that draws us as close as possible, not willing to allow anything to separate us ever again. Until we seize him in worship, we have nothing to convey to others. Listen to the cry of your soul. Grasp the One Who has risen.

Mission (2)

"Then Yeshua said to them, "Do not be afraid; go and take word to My brethren to leave for Galilee, and there they shall see Me." Matthew 28:10

In the middle of this story is an unexpected declaration. "Do not be afraid." Why would Yeshua tell these women not to be afraid? Both women encounter Yeshua after they see the angels in the empty tomb. Yeshua stops them with the greeting, "Joy to you!" They rush to him, clutching his feet and worshipping him. There is no fear here. There is unquenchable joy. There is unwavering devotion. There is inexpressible wonder. So, why does he say, "Do not be afraid"?

What fears might lurk in the minds of these two believers? The obvious one shares the context of the disciples in hiding. Matthew makes it clear that the men were afraid, not because they experienced the overwhelming power of God like Isaiah but because they regarded themselves in mortal danger. If we suppose that Yeshua's comment to these women was comfort intended to remove their personal risk, we have not read the gender correctly. It is the men who hide in fear. These women did not care more for their own well-being than they did for the need to honor their Master in death. They already moved beyond "what about me." Yeshua is not addressing worries about their lives. That was of no concern. These women demonstrated the power of devotion in a way that none of the disciples were able to do. Fear of Roman or Jewish reprisal was not determining their action.

The second possibility is that they were afraid of the power and presence of God. There is a long history of this kind of fear.

When God shows Himself in incredible acts of power, men cower in awe. It is overwhelming to be in the company of the holy God. An experience like that shakes us to our bones. We can remember Peter, James and John when they heard the voice at the transfiguration. They were *afraid*. But this doesn't seem to be the case here. These women already embraced Yeshua. He did not prevent them from grasping him. He spoke tenderly but with incredible news. Be joyful! I am here. Rushing to his feet, they show no hesitation about worshipping him. They know Yeshua. And now, they know him in a new way. They are not afraid of who he is revealed to be. They do not resist their impulse to touch God.

There is another possibility. We might find fear in the anticipation of yet another roller-coaster loss. After all, Yeshua had been taken from them once. What would prevent it from happening again? Perhaps grasping his feet is more than a sign of humble devotion. Perhaps it is that entirely human need for attachment. Once they were powerless to prevent his death. Now they are caught in an emotional whirlwind that demands they grip him for themselves. What parent does not rush to embrace a lost child, not only to express joy but also to secure protection? What man or woman does not cling to one who has come back from near-death in order to shout to the universe, "I will not let you take him again." The motivation behind this fear is possession and protection.

This is the locus of their fear. Yeshua, Lord, do not depart from us again. We cannot go on without you. We seize you to prevent losing you again. We cannot bear the grief another time. If we just grip you tight enough, our lives will be secure in you and, most importantly, we will protect *you* from further harm! These women are acting out emotions associated with the role God designed for them.

How many of us have come to Him in this way? Our lives have been transformed by his touch and we dare not let go. What is this fear? It is the fear that if he should leave us, we would fall back into that choking panic of loss. It is the certain sense that says, "I can only survive when he is right here with me." It is the need to have the guide, the protector and the teacher constantly with us. It is the fear that if he should break contact, I will fail and collapse.

Yeshua allows us to grasp him in worship. He recognizes our need for connection. He knows the fragile web of our emotions. There is fear in our joy. It is the fear that in spite of what we see and touch, it cannot be sustained. It is the fear that this moment of contact with the Master of our souls will evaporate with the morning mist, leaving us once again under the baking sun of a hard life, desolate and desperate. Before Yeshua sends us forth, he reaches into the depths of the fear of joy and comforts us. "I am with you always, even to the close of the age."

Have you grasped the Savior because you were afraid to lose touch with Him? Have you heard yourself say, "I can't go on unless I hold on to you all the time. Don't leave me." The panic fear of being without Him is a step on the path toward service. Without reassurance of companionship, receiving a mission from Him will falter. Yeshua allows us to grasp before we hear Him say, "Don't be afraid." The intensity of our grip will become the intensity of our mission. Holding on is the reciprocal of going out.

Mission (3)

"Then Yeshua said to them, "Do not be afraid; go and take word to My brethren to leave for Galilee, and there they shall see Me." Matthew 28:10

Yeshua spent most of his time being irrelevant. By the world's standards, he wasted most of his effort on the outcasts. He hung around those who were excluded. He healed the ones who did not matter. And most of all, he cared for the largest socially deprived group of the first century – women. He included them in his larger ministry. He taught them. He was sensitive to their traumas, suffering and despair. He was compassionate to them. And some of his deepest revelations about himself and his mission were spoken to women. Without them, the gospel accounts would be sterile.

Women were the first to see the risen Yeshua. Perhaps that's because women were the first to realize the necessity of his death. Perhaps that's because women were the first to identify with His passion. Just as God first revealed to a woman the beginning of the redemptive plan, God first revealed to women the fulfillment of the plan. Yeshua knew women were designed to be the messengers of God's purposes to men, a role established in the creation of the first woman. In their adoration and acceptance, we are all blessed.

Yeshua gives his first commission as the risen Lord to these two women. Their actions demonstrate the faithfulness of a lineage that goes back to Abraham. They believe. So Yeshua says, "Go and take word." It is the abbreviated version of the great commission.

But notice how unusual this mini-commission is. If we were to give the assignment to the two women, we would probably commission them to proclaim the deep theological truths of God's redemption. "Christ has risen. Death is overcome. God has redeemed fallen Mankind. History has changed." The scope of our thoughts would reach toward heaven. And the result would undoubtedly have been a dismal failure. Why? Because Yeshua knew that unless He addressed the present emotional state of these frail human beings, the message would never be heard.

"Go and take word," says the text. In the Greek text the word translated "Go" has the sense of being directed to a particular place. Yeshua does not commission these women to become the bearers of a universal message of forgiveness in His name. He simply asks them to go to the *adelphois* – his beloved brothers who were hiding in fear of their lives. The first commission is local, personal and immediate. Go tell them it is safe. They can travel to Galilee and I will meet them there. He commissions them to do what they are designed to do – proclaim and provide protection for their men. Yeshua does not say one word about the implications of His resurrection. He does not announce divine fulfillment. He did that on the cross at the point of death. Now there is another task to accomplish before the impact of this event will become a message fit for all men. Yeshua must address fear.

These two women show a faith that grows from confusing exuberance to clinging devotion. Now they must move beyond the fear that they will lose Him again to the understanding that He is always with them. They must realize that His physical presence is no longer constrained by time and space. But this realization is not the result of studied philosophical or theological propositions. It is the result of an immediate awareness of His divine presence. Yeshua is God. They see it. They understand at a personal, emotional and volitional level (should we not says "intuitive") that make the need for rational argument unnecessary. He is right here, offering them reassurance.

It is reassurance that Yeshua asks them to carry to the disciples. Yeshua knows that they will report their encounter with the living Lord. But that is not what he wishes them to convey. We would probably have fixed our attention on his presence, on his resurrected reality. But Yeshua knows the heart of Man. He knows that fear will defeat anything we hear in a whirlwind of emotional chaos unless he demonstrates convincingly that we are safely protected in our journey to meet him.

Stop imagining that the disciples were ecstatic over the news. They were nothing but incredulous. They refused to believe. Why? Because they were afraid. The first commission of the resurrected Yeshua is not a command to preach and baptize. It is a request to overcome fear. And women are ideally suited for this commission. They are the protectors. Through the actions of these women we learn something absolutely crucial. Fear comes first! We must deal with fear *before* we can experience resurrection joy.

Are you hiding from the resurrection morning? Is fear clinging to you, preventing you from venturing forward to meet Yeshua? No amount of evidence will overcome those sabotaging emotions until you know that you will be safe. If you are leading others in the name of the Lord, you must begin with the first commission – do not be afraid. As the bearer of good news, the first assignment is the message of safety. When you speak on behalf of the Lord, are your first words, "Do not be afraid"?

FULFILLMENT

Is there more than this?

Women want more, but not always for themselves. In fact, the deepest longing of women is probably focused on the destiny of those they love the most – their husbands and their children. Often the motivation for more is not personal gratification but rather the sheer enjoyment of seeing their loved ones fulfilled. Women seem to have the natural capacity to be advocates, trainers, supporters and motivators. They are gifted with an empathic awareness that few men are able to match. They are designed by God for just this capacity.

But sometimes this natural gift runs ahead of God's purposes. The real test of spiritual maturity in a woman is her willingness to let God direct and domesticate her gift. She is capable of making the best happen for someone else, and often this selfless support of another appears to be noble compassion. But God does not look for compassion alone. He looks for compassion in alignment with His plans. That's the secret – and the difficulty. Eve thought she could be a better "helper" by adding just a bit to her arsenal of abilities. She tried to re-design God's creation. It was a disaster. Everyone faces the same challenge. Will we let God draw the boundaries? In this woman's story, Yeshua confronts the same temptation.

The story of Matthew 20:20-28

"What do you wish?" Matthew 20:21

Every mother wants her children to have the best in life. The mother of James and John was no different. She knew Yeshua represented great power. For the first time in her life, she saw a chance for her sons to leave the life of fishing. A chance for glory. A chance to be lifted out of the daily drudgery and become men of importance. But Yeshua saw something far more serious than a plea for a better life.

When we compare this story with the parallel account in Mark (Mark 10:35 ff.), we find a curious change. Matthew puts the request in the mouth of the mother of these two men, but Mark says that the brothers asked the question directly. By omitting the names of the two sons, Matthew focuses attention on the response of Yeshua rather than the plea. Mark is more revealing, not hiding the manipulation intended by the request. But maybe it takes a bit of both versions to help us learn something from this story.

James and John might well have convinced their mother that Yeshua would be less likely to refuse the request of an elderly woman than two aggressive men. The request is really theirs, but the messenger is chosen to elicit sympathy. It seems like a good tactic. Yeshua's compassion for women was certainly well known by his followers. Yeshua's respect for the elderly could be assumed. Just to make sure that everything is in line for the answer they want, they all come to Yeshua with visible signs of worship. The text says, "bowing down." The word really means "falling." It expresses the position of homage before someone in authority. It is the posture of one who begs.

The drama is not lost on Yeshua. In the only recorded response to the mother, Yeshua acknowledges her intention. "What do you wish?" says that He knows all of this is for an undisclosed purpose. They do not worship out of thanksgiving. This is worship with personal agendas. We should notice that she has yet to say a word. It is her body language that speaks so clearly.

We are the same. Before we say a word, we too often approach the Lord of the universe with some strategy to accomplish our purposes. How many times have we reached for the special verse of Scripture to remind God of His promises (from our perspective)? How often have we mentally reviewed a prayer guaranteed to bring about our desires? Do we seek a crucifix or a special image? Do we look for grace by making a pilgrimage or bowing at a favored shrine? Body language is all too often nothing more than an attempt to bend the will of God in order that it will accommodate the will of Man – of ME! But before we can even open our mouths, Yeshua understands it all. It is motivation, not outward action that determines His response.

"What do you wish?" The text here is clear. Yeshua speaks directly to this woman. It's important to understand the verb used in this question. Greek has two principal verbs for the concept of wish, want or desire. These are *thelema* and *boulomai*. *Thelema* is the verb used to describe not only the purpose to do something but also the actual execution of the intention. It is often used to describe the creative will of God. *Boulomai* expresses deliberate will but not necessarily execution. It is always used to describe the desires and intentions of men. So which word does Yeshua use in his question?

Yeshua understands that the mother of James and John does not come to him with a hopeful plea. She comes with an expectation that he can do whatever he determines to do. Yeshua says, "What do you *thelema* of me?" that is, "What do you expect me to actually accomplish for you?" There is no doubt that power is the issue.

Here is both a positive quality and a negative one. The positive side is revealed in the complete confidence that this woman has in

Yeshua' ability. Although she asks for power for her sons, she has no immediate evidence that Yeshua' kingdom will materialize. Nevertheless, she puts her request to Yeshua because she believes that what He says about His kingdom and what He can accomplish are beyond question. "When you come into your kingdom," not "*If* you come into your kingdom." Her goal might be misdirected, but her confidence is not.

Do we come to Yeshua with assurance that He can do whatever we might ask? Or do we stumble because we second-guess His interest in our hopes? "Yes, I know that Yeshua *can* do anything, but does He *want* to do what I am asking?" My doubt is not about His power. It is about His desire. My faith falters over its understanding of His interest and compassion for me. The mother of James and John teaches us something important. She never doubts His interest or His ability.

But there is another lesson. Yeshua is immune to our manipulations. This woman went through the motions of obeisance in order to accomplish *her* goals. She was far from the kingdom where the citizens serve the Father's goals. "Thy will be done on earth" was not uppermost in her mind. She thought that she could maneuver Yeshua into the right frame of mind so that He would do what *she* wanted done. And this is entirely like us. Our faith is tied to outward and inward contrivances designed to get God to respond to our desires. Act the right way, say the right things, promise the right decisions, read the right words, do whatever it takes to impress God with our sincerity and need so that He will grant what we wish. But Yeshua will have none of this. Before she can say a word, he poses the question, "What are you asking me to completely accomplish for you?" Yeshua does not use subterfuge at all. Straight out with it. Yeshua is not interested in our wishful thinking. He aims straight at the motive – "What do you want *me* to do?"

The only words spoken to the mother of James and John call each of us before the throne. She did not come with the will of the Father in mind. She came with her perspective on life's priorities. And Yeshua asked her if she understood the question correctly. What we ask of Yeshua will be done. There is no break between wish and fulfillment. The verb is *thelema* – a guarantee of completion. So often we come asking without comprehending the consequences of completion. We take the narrow, self-serving view. Yeshua's question places incredible seriousness on such requests. We ask without seeing the long-range picture, but He sees it. So He says, "Have you fully considered how your request fits into the will of the Father? Do you understand that if I do what you ask, there will be eternal consequences? Are you ready for this request to be fully accomplished? Do you really know what you are asking?"

"If you do, then ask – and it shall be given to you. Seek – and you will find. Knock – and I will open the door for you. But count the cost before you come. You are asking from God. Make sure your request has eternal purposes."

CONNECTION

Won't someone help me?

Women are people of community. Deborah Tannen demonstrates that connectedness and community are very early elements in a girl's life, extending not only to family expectations but also to the games and social networks that young girls enjoy. As they grow, relationships and community become stronger and stronger parts of life's fabric. In some senses, the current culture's attempt to force equality in the marketplace carries the unfortunate consequence of replacing a woman's connectedness with the much more sterile and isolated world of men. Women know how to care for others and this translates directly into their natural ability to connect. Where there is a thriving community, you will usually find women at the heart.

Of course, this ability and need to connect carries an equally significant negative side. A woman forced into isolation will not simply be alone. She will be disconnected from her true self. She was designed to be in relationship. To push her out of the circle is to sentence her to terminal discouragement. Yeshua meets such a woman and in the same day, connects her to someone who shares this life and death encounter.

The story of Mark 5:21-24 and 35-43

"Talitha kum!" Mark 5:41

Tucked into the corner of the story about the woman with the hemorrhage is a remarkable vignette. A child is brought back to life. Twelve years old. Hardly a woman by our standards but in first century Palestine, in a few months she would be of marriageable age. Mark includes this detail in order to place responsibility with the parents. The father comes to Yeshua to ask for the life of his daughter. Before this day is done, Yeshua asks something of them in return.

Recall the woman who suffered from a twelve-year hemorrhage. Her desperate plight began the same year that this child was born. While her life eroded into torment, poverty and ostracism, this child grew toward acceptance as a member of the community. Now, on the same day, crisis will connect them both. Yeshua's delay caused by the woman who grasped his robe resulted in the death of this child. While one was being brought back into the community, the other left. New life for one meant death for the other.

The healing of the woman with a hemorrhage is really an interruption in the story of Jarius' daughter. Jarius, a member of the religious leadership, comes to Yeshua with a plea to lay hands on his daughter and save her from certain death. But on the way, servants of the household report that she has already died. There is no use in making the trip now. Yeshua is undisturbed. With three disciples he continues to the home. When he arrives, funeral preparations are underway. Yeshua questions the commotion, saying, "The child has not died, but is asleep." This statement is greeted with ridicule. The funeral party laughs at Yeshua. "Asleep? Are you crazy? Ah, but of course you are. You're that *prophet* who claims to do miracles. Well, you're too late for this one. Better luck next time."

The Greek text tells us that Yeshua "put them out." The words are emphatic and direct. "Get out!" Faithlessness before the messenger of El Shaddai is tantamount to blasphemy. Yeshua sends them away because they have excluded themselves from the mercy God is about to display. Only the parents and the three disciples are allowed to observe God's intervention.

Before we jump to the conclusion of this story, it is important to notice the emotional climate. This family has been on the roller coaster of pain. Their only daughter becomes gravely ill – the nightmare of every parent. With visible expression of faith, they seek Yeshua, believing that he is able to save her. Yeshua agrees and the mood swings upward. There is hope. But on the way, another woman delays Yeshua, a woman whose need disrupts the progress that Jarius believes is essential. This is not part of the plan, so much so that even Yeshua is not aware of the identity of this woman. Jarius must have been stricken with anxiety the moment Yeshua stopped, uttering those words, "Who touched me?" Jarius' plans and hopes were suspended, hanging by a thread while the interrupter confronted Yeshua. Then the train begins again, but before it can reach the destination, the news arrives. "Your daughter has died." What does Jarius think now? Does he still rejoice in the cure for the hemorrhaging woman or does he harbor resentment toward her?

"Why did she get in the way? Why, God? If we had only continued without her, my daughter would be saved. But now, what? Why save her at the expense of my child?"

Is there any parent who would not think this way? God diverted is God absent. A moment too late to rescue might as well be an eternity. Death reigns supreme. Jarius is plummeting toward the bottom of the arc. The blood rush. The stomach churn. Face against the inevitable.

But Yeshua never hurries. Lesson number one: God always has enough time to fulfill His plans. When Abraham thought God was forty years too late, El Shaddai said to him, "Is anything too difficult for Me?" Yeshua knows that the Ruler of the universe is also the Lord of time. "Do not fear, only believe."

What is your sense of the temporally expedient? Yeshua understood perfectly God's unhurried intersections with men. He also knew that the normal response to disruption would be faltering faith. Reassurance is required. Even if the leader sees the vision of God's intention, awareness of human frailty must be considered. Fear is capable of overcoming any follower.

I often stand with Jarius at this moment in his journey. I know that Yeshua is the Lord of life, but my horizon is bound by the tyranny of the present. Some intruder, some unexpected need or concern disrupts my life with my Rescuer. In my haste to follow, I let *my* map of the journey become the measure of the journey's success. And suddenly God moves in another direction. Recall this important element of the interruption in Jarius' program. Yeshua did not *plan* to heal the woman with the hemorrhage. God did, through His Son, without His Son's intention. Yeshua was going one way. God took a short detour. But our versions of detours are not obstacles to God. He has *all the time necessary* to accomplish His will. His view is always *thelema* – intention accompanied by completion.[9]

Yeshua's leadership embraced the interruption as God's redirection. Yeshua did not panic, regroup, withdraw, reevaluate or

---

[9] See *thelema* in this book under the chapter on FULFILLMENT

become unnerved. God doesn't have the same temporal constraints that we do. But He is never late. If we are going to see the Yeshua who led Jarius, we will have to see a Yeshua who understood that redirection is the press of God's thumb on life. Every intersection is divine backdrop for obedience.

Whose clock runs your life?

CONNECTION (2)

"Talitha kum!" Mark 5:41

Yeshua enters the room of the dead girl. It is very quiet now. The mourners have been sent away. The parents stand in the shadows. Father comforts Mother as she weeps, his arms around her shaking body. The front of her garment shows the signs of recent kneeling on the dirt floor. The man is resolute, holding back the tears in his effort to believe even here. James, John and Peter stand near the doorway, watching. The air is heavy and still. A shaft of light catches the swirling galaxies of dust flickering into life with photon reflections. Outside a bird sings one of God's shorter symphonies. In spite of the afternoon heat around the window, the corners of the room have a musty, damp feel.

Yeshua approaches the mat where the child's body lies. The skin is still damp from the fever. But the face is a porcelain mask, blanched and distant. Yeshua pauses. As though in slow motion, all of the eyes in the room follow the movement of Yeshua's hand as he reaches for the child. His hand overwhelms the tiny hand of this small victim. It is strong from years of woodwork. It is weathered from years of exposure. It is dusty from the road. But the movement is so full of compassion and grace that there is no doubt at all – it is God's hand. The small fingers disappear, folded under the hand that is an angel's wing.

"Talitha kum." "Little girl, arise." When Yeshua called Lazarus from the tomb, the text tells us that he cried out in a loud voice, "Come forth!" But volume did not drive death away. He cried out because he wanted no one to be confused about what was happening and who was causing it to happen. His shout was for those who observed. The English translation of his Aramaic

command here does not require an exclamation[10]. In fact, as we shall see, Yeshua is not ready to reveal what happens here to anyone except those whom he invites. There is no need to cry out. Why would you wake a child with a shout? I can imagine Yeshua leaning forward. A whisper from his lips. "Rise up, little one." It is tender, gentle. The way any loving father would wake up his only child. "Open your eyes. See. Things are fine. I'm right here. You're safe now." Isn't that what we would say?

Death's grip is not broken by force. It is broken by love. The only two words spoken to this child are words of love. And because they are words of love, they are the most powerful words she could ever hear.

Mark tells us that immediately she got up and began walking. Perfectly healthy. We need to pay attention to the action. She does not *recover*. She gets up and goes about being a twelve-year-old as if nothing had happened. Put aside the video images of morphing back to life. This is instantaneous, miraculous genesis. This is God, not MGM. Mark's inclusion of the word *periepatei* (walked) deliberately shows us how normal she is. So normal that Yeshua reminds the observers she will be hungry and needs some breakfast.

And now the secret. Yeshua orders all who see to not tell anyone about what happened. The word Mark uses is *diesteilato*. This is

---

[10] The Greek here is *legei*, meaning "says." The reason that this expression has the added exclamation point is due to the parallel passage in Luke 8:54 where the Greek is *ephonese legon* ("he called, saying"). The idea of an exclamation is found in the Greek root *phoneo*. While this word can be translated with exclamatory nuances (the crow of a rooster Matt. 26:34, the blare of a trumpet Amos 3:6), it is also translated as simply "call, speak, invite or name" (cf. John 2:9, Luke 14:12 and John 13:13). Consider the context. Yeshua does not wish others to know what is happening. He is also very aware of the needs of this child. Does the context suggest a shout or simply a tender address?

in the middle voice indicating that it has special significance for the subject. This is very important, says Yeshua. Don't spread the news.

Do you think that the resurrection of this girl could be contained? Of course not. As soon as she stepped outside the house, people would know. Who does Yeshua really address in this command? Probably not the three disciples. They were quite sure to recount the event to the other disciples. Yeshua is directing his exhortation to the parents but he knows that soon the whole village will discover the truth. Why would he say such a thing? The answer is simple. Yeshua wants to leave before the news spreads. It is God's glorification, not his. He does not want a crowd crowing credit. He came to heal a small girl. That was all.

How many of us reflect the humility of this man? How many of us send away the crowds, accomplish God's intentions, and slip out the back? Don't we often "spotlight" people instead. Post the pictures with the President. Frame the degrees. Run the headlines (which we keep in a scrap book), smile for the camera. Look, God, at what I did for you. Aren't you proud of how I handled this situation?

Yeshua is the silent leader. His leadership shows in the life (literally) of others. While he walks at the front of the group, it is not for fame and glory. He is at the front because the point man takes the biggest risk. He will be the first to face the enemy and die. And when victory happens, he takes up the rear. Yeshua does not look for medals or plaques. He looks for tiny hands that need to be lifted up. If you follow this man, you will often find ways to slip out the back before the party begins. Your job is over when God is glorified.

CONNECTION (3)

"Talitha kum!" Mark 5:41

We have learned quite a bit about the character of being a servant-leader from these two words. There is one more lesson here. It is the lesson of the *magic words*. It is not a lesson intended for those who witnessed this miracle. It is a lesson for the rest of us.

When we read this story, one of the things that strikes us is that fact that Mark and Luke include the Aramaic phrase in their Greek texts. This is not their usual practice. In fact, there are only a few occasions where Aramaic is transliterated into the New Testament. We see it when Yeshua addresses his Father as *Abba* and when Yeshua quotes Psalm 22:1 from the cross. Matthew's account of this miracle mentions neither the Aramaic phrase nor the exhortation to secrecy. This is all the more unusual because neither Mark nor Luke witnessed the miracle. Peter did. It is commonly believed that Peter was Mark's primary source for his material and that Luke borrowed material from Mark (and probably talked to Peter) when he wrote. So, the source of this recollection is probably Peter.

But Peter would not view this sentence as unusual at all. Peter spoke Aramaic. They all did. What makes it unusual is not what happened on that day, but why it was kept in the original language. And that presents us with a subtle but deadly mistake. We might unintentionally think that these were special words.

Faith is the combination of the mysterious and the sublimely rational. We will never understand the full workings of the Father and the Spirit in the process of redemption and renewal. Faith contains, as Paul reminds us, a great mystery. But just as this mystery conceals some of God's handiwork, God has also chosen to reveal great portions of His plans. Faith is not blind. It is the most reasonable, logical and confirmed truth we have. God's character embraces truth and truth just makes sense. It is sin that is illogical and irrational.

Nevertheless, the mysterious element of faith has driven many to imagine interaction with God as the realm of secrets. In the first century, there were many Greek mystery religions. They survived because they claimed to have "secret knowledge" about the workings of the universe, much like astrologers and mystics do today. There is a built-in appeal about secrets. Secrets elevate those who know into the category of the elite, the initiated. Secrets bait the trap of arrogance. I know something you don't; therefore I am better than you.

The history of human religions is filled with magical secrets. If we are not very careful, we will fall victim to this seduction. We will begin to use "special" words, power words, as though they contained power in themselves. "In the name of Jesus." How often have we heard that phrase proclaimed as though it were mystical ointment insuring success? "Jehovah-Jireh" has become a popular power expression. Then there is "In the name of the Father, the Son and the Holy Ghost" and "By the power of His name." The "name it and claim it" heresy. They are all wonderful words, but not a single one is specially endowed. It is not the words that matter. It is the person behind the words. We use power words to make ourselves powerful. But Yeshua knew that powerful people are far from humble servants.

We have already discovered that Yeshua's leadership meant stepping out of the limelight. God was glorified while Yeshua slipped away to the next assignment. As his followers, we may recognize this requirement. But how easy it is to let the words become our pathway to glory instead. How many leaders retain their power through secrets? How often have we been guilty of managing information in order to control? Are we ready to let our words be just the ordinary stuff of life, offered up to God for His use? Or are we looking for a way to bolster self-image by arrogant aggrandizement of the facts?

Yeshua is not the author of secret words of power. He is not a Saturday morning cartoon superhero with mystical energy. Yeshua is *the* Servant Leader, the one who understands the deepest meaning of personal humility. The one who is tied to those in need with the greatest of all bonds – the words of love. Yeshua is the leader who does not need the credit and who does not offer the quotations. Yeshua knows that it's not about him. It's about the glory of God. God's way is to just slip out the back.

WORRY

What if something terrible happens?

Women worry. It's just part of the job of caring about others. They might not worry more than men, but they certainly worry about things men don't seem to be aware of. Most of the time, they worry about what might happen to someone else. Maybe that's why we hear stories of the extraordinary courage women display when someone else is in trouble. They seem to think of themselves *after* everyone else is safe. Of course, concern about others is a good thing. God makes us the object of His concern, and it's a very good thing that He does. But concern and worry aren't quite the same.

There was a day very early in Yeshua's life when worry and concern came face-to-face. How he responded to his mother helps all of us recognize the difference – and the difference it makes.

The story of Luke 2:41-51

"Why is it that you were looking for Me? Did you not know that I had to be in My Father's house?" Luke 2:49

Gap Kids seemed like just the right store. My three-year-old daughter, the youngest and the only girl, tagged right alongside me. I thought, "Oh, my. Wouldn't she look so cute in that Easter dress and hat?" Taking her by the hand, we walked in among the other shoppers. The store was busy, but we soon found just the right black velour dress and matching hat. She looked adorable when I held it up in front of her. "Yes, this is it."

Up to the counter, child in one hand, clothes in the other. A line at the counter, then finally, our turn. I put down the clothes, let go of Rachel and reached for my wallet. I turned to the clerk and gave the credit card. "ID, please," she said. I looked down at the pockets in the wallet, found the right laminated piece of plastic and delivered it. When my hand was free, I reached for Rachel. I grasped air.

In one microsecond, my world imploded. Rachel was gone. I turned completely around, running my eyes over a sweep of the surroundings. No Rachel! The adrenaline was pumping now, flashes in the corner of my eyes. The clerk looked confused.

As quickly as I could I said, "My three-year-old has disappeared. Wait." I ran to the door that opened into the mall. Second story. I thought, "falling." What if she fell? But she was not outside. So I did the only thing I could think of. I stood up on one of the mannequin displays and shouted to everyone in the store, "My three-year-old is somewhere in this store. Help me find her. Please."

Dozens of mothers immediately started looking. Under one of the racks sat Rachel, calming playing with a button she found on the floor. Oblivious of her father's panic. Content to just enjoy her game.

Anyone who has ever gone through an experience like that, or worse, will know exactly what Mary and Joseph felt when they discovered that Yeshua was not with the traveling group. Their exasperated panic shows itself in the language they use when they finally locate him.

"Why did you do this to us? Your father and I have been looking everywhere for you. We were very upset."

Mary's declaration is probably quite restrained. Can you imagine how you would feel? Of course she is upset. But the emphasis is on the question, "Why did you do this to us?" The responsibility is placed entirely on Yeshua. His action caused their problem.

This claim makes Yeshua's reply all the more startling. "Why did you look for me?" Can you imagine any parent *not* looking for a lost child? They are amazed at his response. From Yeshua' perspective, he is doing what he is supposed to do. He is being responsible to the guidance of his Father. But the perspective of those around him is entirely different.

This story forces some difficult choices. Are we to say that Yeshua was right in his assessment? Is he excused from an act that would have any parent in the world in a frenzy simply because he is the Christ? If Yeshua is fulfilling the Father's will, does this lay aside the responsibility to inform others?

If this story were not about a twelve-year-old, we would answer these questions with ease. Leaders often have to go in a direction that is not apparent to others, sometimes without communicating the consequences of following their vision. We confidently assert the need to follow God's will no matter what the results. The difficulty is not with the actual dialogue but rather with the emotions and expectations. And that is the direct result of our misapprehension of God's care.

We understand Mary's question because we completely identify with the human perspective. "Why didn't you tell me what you were going to do?" We have this need to know. We even make these demands on God. "Father, why don't you tell me what You are doing in these circumstances?" or less politely with Job, "God, give me an answer here." Our field of vision is limited by the confidence that we place in His care. Even Mary, who had substantial evidence that God's hand was on her son, fell victim to the limits of the human horizon. She did not consider God's protection in this drama.

"Why did you do this to us?" But what precisely did Yeshua do? Who is really responsible for the distress? Years later Yeshua would tell the listeners, "Do not be anxious for your life." Is he recalling the anxiety of his mother's words? He points out that anxiety is *my* decision to take God's sovereign control of life onto my shoulders. Mary has forgotten something important, not just about this special child, but about all of God's creation. She is not free from anxiety because she has not yet come to see the incredible, meticulous, intentional care of God. Her reaction is a perfectly human reaction. And that is precisely why it surprises Yeshua.

"Mother, don't you know who cares for me?" It isn't a reprimand. It is a genuinely puzzled question from the mouth of an innocent child. Don't children often surprise us with their intuitive depth of faith? They are free of the anxiety that characterizes adults because they truly believe that the responsibility for life's care belongs to someone else. I sat in my office, writing about the struggle of my faith in crisis. My eleven-year-old daughter sat next to me, aimlessly playing with a rubber band. This disparity forced a question.

"Rachel, don't you worry about what is going to happen to you and stuff like that?"

She looked at me with an expression of complete surprise and sincerity. "No."

Oh, what freedom to be a child, confident in the arms of the Father!

My anxiety is like Mary's, deeply rooted in a mistrust of God's world. Yeshua's response does not scorn my concern. It is not a concern for the life of my child. It is the concern that overtakes fears about *me*! Yeshua's response helps me see that I am blinded by my efforts to be the god of my life. It is an expression that only a child could make – one who has yet to be *un*educated about reality, one who hasn't yet be taught the human mythology of self-reliance. Mary certainly was concerned about the well-being of her son. That's what it means to be a mother. But when that concern gets transferred to my own life and to the control that I want to exercise over the lives of others, I need to step back. I need to recognize that trust in God is the root of all obedience – and all confidence.

For those of us who wish to represent the character of Yeshua in this world of human anxiety, a certain quizzical element must enter our view of the care of life. It's not surprising that human beings doubt God's complete control. Human beings are obsessed with control issues. But Yeshua tells us that those who participate in the kingdom of God's reign will adopt a childlike attitude. And the truth children plainly see is that life is not in their hands. They don't try to control their world because it is so obvious to them that they can't. They simply trust.

Do we?

WORRY (2)

"Why is it that you were looking for Me? Did you not know that I had to be in My Father's house?" Luke 2:49

If we have discovered that the root of anxiety is on our side of the divine-human equation, we will recognize Yeshua's childlike question for what it is. Shock and surprise that what is so clearly obvious to him is not so clearly obvious to others. Trust in the Father is the paramount attitude of faith. And trust excludes anxiety.

Yeshua's second question reveals the other side of the coin.

Mary and Joseph are a day's journey from Jerusalem when they discover Yeshua is missing. After an incredibly fretful night, they start back to the city. Another day of travel. They arrive at dusk. There is no sense beginning the search now. Soon there will be no light. So, a second night passes with worry and concern. On the third day, as soon as the sun is up, they begin scouring the streets of Jerusalem, looking for this wayward twelve-year-old. They undoubtedly searched the most familiar places first. Eventually they arrive at the temple, the center of the festival they had attended days before.

The temple of Solomon is imposing. There are alcoves and porticos and out of the way corners where people gather for worship, prayer and teaching. The morning light filters through the windows high above, throwing angled ladders of illumination across the rooms. Mary and Joseph hurry from one spot to another, eyes darting back and forth, when suddenly, there he is. But instead of cowering in a corner, lost and afraid, he is sitting among the scribes and the teachers, quietly conversing, completely at ease.

Yeshua's second question is about the *scope* of our commitment. But if we look deeper into this verse, we will find something unusual. The word "house" in this verse is not really there at all. By inserting it, we might get the idea that there is part of life that is God's and part that is ours. What a mistake! Literally, the Greek says, "I must be *in My Father's these*." It is a very unusual sentence. We add other words to make sense of it in English. Perhaps we are too anxious to fill in the gaps. Perhaps what Yeshua is saying is considerably deeper than we imagine a twelve-year-old might say.

This is a verse that requires the context in order to complete. It is a thought that embraces openness toward life because it refuses to partition God's world. Yeshua does not say that he must be in God's house in opposition to what is outside God's house. The context of the *first* question shows us that for Yeshua, God rules *all* of life's houses. God's business is not restricted to any particular place.

Do we have a *spiritual* part of life and a separate *business* part of life? Does Yeshua give you advice on your P&L? Does He interview your new hires? Is He there at the planning table? Does He sit with you on the school board? Is He at your dinner table, in the children's classroom, at the gym?

If we take this statement of Yeshua and fill in the missing word with anything that pushes us in the direction of partition, we will be tempted to see commitment as "part" of life, the part that Yeshua committed to his Father's house or his Father's affairs. But what if we read the verse as it is? What if we recognize that it is a statement about existence, not a statement about partitions? The meaning of this odd Greek construction must be supplied from the context and that context shows us that Yeshua was surprised that anyone wouldn't see God's total concern with everything in life. That is exactly how we should look at our own servant leader lives. We need to let God supply the meaning to our lives from the context – His context.

There are no partitions in the life of a servant leader. There is only "my Father's these." All of who I am is about what God wants. The context of my life supplies the meaning of the phrase "the Father's these" for me. Are you living your Father's "these" or are you managing your life from your own context? If you look at your behavior, who's really in control?

BLESSING

Why can't I be the lucky one?

Everyone wants to be blessed. The good life – yes, that's the goal. But for most of us, life is just what it is. Routine. Hard. Sprinkled with bits of joy. Mixed with portions of sorrow. Shaken with regrets. Hopefully, with a good measure of love. It's a drink we might not choose – if we had a choice. But we don't, do we? So we make the best of the hand we are dealt. Sometimes it seems pretty good. Sometimes we can't even draw a pair.

Then there are the lucky ones. They seem to have everything we want, effortlessly. Their lives are elevated. Somehow they don't have to trod the same streets, work the same jobs, deal with the same problems. They move among us detached from the ordinary. We're not quite sure how all this happens, but it doesn't seem to happen to us. For us, luck is nothing more than the result of extra work or longer hours. It's luck we *make*, not luck we get.

The Greek New Testament uses the word *makarios* when Yeshua speaks about blessings. The word is associated with good fortune and luck. Maybe Yeshua knows the secret of good luck. For women who carry such heavy loads, a blessing from Yeshua would be a nice relief. He gives just this kind of blessing to an unnamed woman. But it turns out to be not what we expected.

The story of Luke 11:27-28

But he said, "On the contrary, blessed are those who hear the word of God, and observe it." Luke 11:28

All she meant to do was compliment his upbringing. Such a fine son! So intelligent. So charismatic. It was enough to make any mother proud.

The crowd pushed and shoved as people maneuvered themselves to gain the best vantage points. But she was not strong enough to hold her own ground. She realized she would not get the chance to pat his arm and tell him what a fine job he was doing. But she was not going to be denied praising him. So she blurted it out.

"Happy is the womb that bore you and the breasts that fed you."

What better compliment could be given? Lineage was so much a part of the thinking of the Jews. Yeshua was just the kind of son any mother would want. And he was becoming quite a popular figure. There is nothing better than success to bless a poor family. Yes, his mother surely would be beaming with pride over this result.

The crowd probably concurred. Yeshua was no stranger to them. They heard the reports. He healed people. He fed thousands from nothing. There is even a rumor that he could raise the dead. And those closest to him seem to be able to do miraculous things too. Hadn't seventy followers just come back with wonderful news? The movement was growing. Wherever Yeshua went, the news of his arrival brought excitement. Expectation was high. What would he do next? In spite of the oppression of the Romans and the hard life of Palestine, it was a thrill to be alive today. Today the prophet from Nazareth was here.

As soon as the old woman exclaimed her praise, the heads of those in the crowd must have nodded in agreement. After all, Yeshua is one of us. He is the local boy whom God has certainly anointed. He is going to be great – and we are going to be his followers, brought to victory behind him. Yes, she's right. What a blessing he must be to his family! How fortunate they are to be able to claim him as their own.

We are not so different from this woman in the crowd. We stand in awe of our leaders, offering praises to them for their brilliance, vision and abilities. Men and women who are models of success. We stand admiring, sharing in the limelight. And, of course, we use our association with these great figures to name-drop status for ourselves.

"Oh, I know him." "Yes, I worked for her." "He's one of my friends." "I was in a meeting with her just yesterday."

It's so easy to make the connection. It's part of the acceptable form of pride. It gives us status. We are on the inside with the big shots.

Yeshua immediately corrects this tangent. His course is not about status, for others in association with him or for himself.

"On the contrary, blessed are those who hear the word of God, and observe it." The Greek text opens this statement with *menounge*. The word translating Yeshua's Hebrew expression tells us something quite different. It is a combination of *men* (indeed), *oun* (but or now or therefore) and *ge* (a particle that expresses emphasis). This word is not always translated "on the contrary." In fact, in Romans 10:18 and Philippians 3:8, the sense of the word is enthusiastic *agreement*, not emphatic denial. Only the context can determine the meaning.

Yeshua is not denying His mother's happiness. The emotions she felt regarding him are some of the highest human blessings. No compliment means more to a parent than to have someone praise your child. But this woman's shout of praise is far too restrictive for God's view of happiness. Yeshua does not act to please his mother. He acts to redefine the scope of happiness. The woman in the crowd saw happiness as an external relation, available to a few through lucky heritage or good upbringing. Yeshua sees happiness as an internal relation, available to everyone through obedience. Everyone who does the will of God is truly happy. This woman's blessing upon *the womb that bore you* (the mother) is exclusive. It leaves most of the world out. But Yeshua's blessing is inclusive. All may enjoy its benefit. God never plays favorites.

How many of us are ready to accept both facets of this correction? Have we moved beyond our narrowly defined version of blessing, allowing God's handiwork through us to become the lucky intersection for anyone who comes? Or are we still holding up the banner of having the right label, being in the right line, knowing the right people? Yeshua widens our view. Anyone who hears the call and obeys is welcome to enjoy the blessing.

In our efforts to influence others, are we leaders who willingly set aside praises and complements because they detract from the mission to serve? Or do we discover a sympathetic harmony when others recognize how wonderful we are? Do we love the accolades and the spotlight? The servant of the Lord began life in a stall for animals. Perhaps we need to be more in touch with straw when we begin to feel proud of our position.

BLESSING (2)

But he said, "On the contrary, blessed are those who hear the word of God, and observe it." Luke 11:28

Happiness for all. But there is still a condition, isn't there? Yeshua corrects the praise of the woman in the crowd. Happiness is not limited to the luck of a good birth or an exemplary family. Happiness is for everyone who hears the word of God – *and keeps it*.

The verb for "keeps it" is *phulasso*. It's about guard duty. The flavor of Yeshua's thought is not simply following the edicts of God's word, but also standing guard over this word. When we obey, we do more than align our actions with God's will. We also *endorse and protect* the integrity of God's purposes. We become the living sanctuary of God's word, a place where God's honor and character are protected and cherished.

Happy are those who hear what God's says and become guardians of His character.

God invites everyone to happiness. The invitation is unconditional. God doesn't care if you are from the palace or the stable. He doesn't care if you are the best or the worst. He doesn't care about your bloodline or your background. You are not invited on the basis of your worthiness. You are invited because He **decides** to invite you. But the invitation has an RSVP. Yeshua is not ambiguous about the demands that fall on those who follow him. Yeshua is not a spokesman for tolerance. He is quite clear. Unless you respond to the RSVP, the invitation will have no affect on you.

Did you *hear* the invitation to happiness in God's word? Great! That invitation went out to everyone. Now look at the bottom of the card. RSVP – accept this invitation by entering into God's guard duty.

The woman in the crowd who shouted a blessing for Yeshua' mother understood part of the meaning of *makarios*, the Greek word for "happy." Happiness is a function of relationship. What she did not understand is that the relationship is not physical. It is spiritual. Happiness is a result of standing guard for God.

We are familiar with Yeshua's famous blessings called the Beatitudes. They are not what we usually imagine. Typically, we think the blessings of the Beatitudes are something we receive as a result of some spiritual practice or condition, just as this woman believed that Mary's blessing was the result of good genes and obedience. But the Beatitudes, including this one, are not *blessings you receive*. They are descriptions about being happy. They are not about what we get from practicing spiritual disciplines. They are about how we react to what life hands us. That is the real sense of *makarios*. It means "lucky," "fortunate" or "happy." It is not a verb like "to be blessed." It is an adjective. Those *happy* ones. Yeshua moves the focus from the singular announcement of the woman in the crowd to the plural inclusion of all those who hear and obey. Those who hear and obey are happy, lucky and fortunate, not because they inherit a blessing but because happiness is the nature of obedience.

There are many beatitudes in the Bible. The pattern runs from Genesis to Revelation. These "blessing" statements reveal God's view of happiness. In this verse, Yeshua provides a penetrating insight. Happiness is not about what I have, what I want or what I can acquire. Happiness is found in obedience to my Lord.

The practical apostle James tells us to be doers of the word and not hearers only. He is only reflecting the teaching of his half-brother. We search for happiness with the wrong map. Happiness lies right in front of us. There is no secret to it at all. Just do what God says. That's it. Nothing more is required. Happiness is about a relationship of servitude. It is calling "Lord, Lord" (a request for instruction) and then doing what He says.

Leaders intuitively know the truth in Yeshua's insight. Followers are happy when they *hear* the word of the leader and *do* what is required. That insight places two critical responsibilities on the leader. The first is to communicate the word so that it will be heard. That is not a statement about volume. Louder does not mean better. It is a statement about transmitting comprehension. If you are not understood, no one will be able to follow. Yeshua spent three years communicating through his words, his actions, his emotions, his sacrifice and his prayers. After three years of day-in and day-out communicating, most of his disciples still did not understand. But He never gave up until enlightenment arrived, even though he had to die first.

The second responsibility of the leader is to be a doer too. Yeshua led by doing. His happiness came by obeying the Father in everything. No servant leader of the Master will be effective without obedience, the same obedience that calls all who follow.

Do you want happiness to flood your life? Stop looking in all the wrong places. Obey what you know **now**. That's enough to get going.

DESTINY

What was I made for?

Today women face questions their mothers never thought about. For centuries the world simply assumed that women were destined to bear children, care for the home and serve their husbands. Now women face questions about careers, social commitments, relationships and children. The assumptions that governed a woman's choices no longer seem to apply. Now it's a question of destiny.

Everyone would like to know life's game plan. How much easier it would be to know in advance why I was born, why I am here and what I was destined to become. We struggle to understand who we are and how we fit in the world. For women, that struggle is complicated by the erosion of typical expectations. Perhaps we can find some clues for resolving this burden if we look closely at Yeshua's perspective on life's destiny. It all comes into focus in a brief encounter with the women who watched Him carry the cross to His death.

The story of Luke 23:27-31

"Daughters of Jerusalem, stop weeping for Me, but weep for yourselves and for your children." Luke 23:28

If we are able to break through the barriers of self-absorbed living, we are confronted with the agony of this world. Perhaps the enormity of the world's genuine suffering is the motivation for not looking. We are Greek in our unredeemed souls. Greek philosophy taught that sympathy for the overwhelming suffering of the innocent was something to fear, not encourage. Why? Because the presence of undeserved suffering in another human being forces me to confront the possibility that I might suffer in the same way. Better to pretend immunity than to deal with a heart torn between trauma and dread. Better to censor the news images than face the reality of human evil.

Luke tells us that there were women along the steps to Golgotha who were overwhelmed by the torture of Yeshua. The words used to describe their trauma are "wailing" and "lamenting." We don't hear these words often so we need to bring them a little closer to home. Violence perpetrates violence, even in sympathy. Greek has three words that describe outward emotional displays of grief. These words are progressively more violent, from inner grief and tears to visible bodily reaction to physical abuse of one's own body as a sign of deep disturbance. Luke uses the second and third stages in the two words he chooses. The words Luke uses describe women who are beating themselves with their own fists in agonizing empathy. One word even suggests cutting the body as a display of grief. All the while, these women were venting their emotions with cries and screams. Forget the pictures of silent tears and shuddering shoulders. Replace your images with women who are collapsing outwardly and inwardly in the face of despicable evil. When they see what has happened to Yeshua, they want to tear themselves apart just as their hearts are being torn apart. They are beyond words. To witness his torment is to fall to the ground, devastated, helpless and destroyed.

Have you ever faced this kind of emotional overload? Most of us have come no closer than seeing an actor in a movie pretend to vomit at the sight of a dead body. But life is not MGM. If we let go of the protective screen sheltering us from the agony of others, we discover that there are soul connections we never wished to acknowledge.

September 11. A nation shattered with grief. Many of us wailed and lamented over senseless slaughter of innocent lives. The door of communal agony was opened for a glimpse of the rest of the world's everyday reality. Rwanda, Kazakhstan, North Korea, Bosnia – the list could go on and on. Racial genocide, ethnic cleansing, political oppression – it doesn't matter what you call it. Extermination and torture are the hallmarks of human aggression. One or one million, the picture of human suffering is the same. Evil has human eyes.

How does Yeshua respond to this cry of soul identification? He points toward a deeper reality still to come. His vision is not what's happening at that moment. It is a vision of what will happen later as a result of that moment.

"Daughters of Jerusalem" – the phrase invokes tenderness from the lips of a man being beaten, tortured and executed. Here is the precursor to "Forgive them because they do not know what they are doing." Yeshua's heart reaches toward those who are suffering with his agony, not to elicit sympathy, but to give warning. The man who is being broken before them is offering them a gift birthed in his own suffering. Be careful. This event before you marks the Day of Judgment for the world.

"Do not weep over me," says Yeshua. The verb is intense to match the expressions of these women. They can see the agony in front of them, but they are blind to the real horror of this moment. God is separating the world over the line of the cross. These women are grieving because one of their own is being led to his death, but they do not see that his death will lead to the destruction of all who are blind before His Father.

We are quick to acknowledge that following Yeshua means laying our lives down for others. We rationally assent to this ultimate call to the fellowship of his suffering. But do we really believe that we are called to die for those who hate our message? Are we stabbed to the heart over their blindness? Leadership is the incubator of sympathetic acceptance. How easy it is to let others weep over us, over our trials, over our struggles, over our commitment. How seductive it is to replace God's weeping over the lost with the lost weeping over us. Every leader is subject to the accolades of sympathy, even in torment and trial. And every leader must carefully examine ego at a moment when ego is so susceptible to personal acknowledgement. "Yes, I am suffering for them. I deserve their sympathy." Yeshua will not allow it. Even in suffering the human heart has the deceptive power to turn to self-glorification.

When Yeshua turns to these women, he is not reprimanding them. He does not tell them their agonizing sympathy is wrong. He simply points beyond the visible horizon. The tragedy is not the present torture and crucifixion. The tragedy is rejection of God's Messiah. That is worth lament. It breaks the heart of God.

Yeshua teaches a powerful message here. It is a message that is borne on the wings of horror and because it is surrounded by horror, we can easily lose sight of the real lesson. A servant leader acts for the glory of God, even when the entire world turns to glorify the leader. What more natural setting to accept the glorification of self than in our deepest agonies? A martyr's death. A bruised and beaten heroine. Our hearts are moved, and they should be. But there is a much deeper reality. God's glory is in the cross, whether on Golgotha or in my own backyard. It is His glory, not mine. And I must be very careful to guard myself from falling into exalting myself in a "deserving" moment.

Destiny (2)

"Daughters of Jerusalem, stop weeping for Me, but weep for yourselves and for your children." Luke 23:28

Is it a warning or a proclamation of great compassion? On the surface, we might hear a warning. "Don't weep for me. I am not the one who will really suffer the consequences of this event. You, Jewish mothers, will see God's hand punish you and your children because you have rejected me." There is truth in this warning. Yeshua would die that day. His death liberated those who heard his message. These Jews did not understand his purpose. They could not imagine a suffering Messiah. They judged themselves because they refused to believe.

But they still wept over him. They wept because *pathos* gripped them. To see the inhumanity of men toward another man, to witness the stark reality of human brutality is more than enough for any mother of any son to fall to her knees in agonizing shock. It is the *pathos* of human connection – mother and child linked by blood and body.

Yeshua understood that *pathos*. He knew the feelings of a vital relationship ripped away. He knew what it was like to weep over those who were about to be lost. The word is *klaio*. Its heritage is significant. This word is often associated with the grief we experience in repentance.[11] It is the precursor to God's saving grace. But it is also used to express the pain and emotion of those who discover they are lost under the wrath of God. This word is used once to describe Yeshua's *pathos*. It is not where we would expect it to be.

---

[11] Remember the previous studies, "Remorse" and "Grief" where the same word is employed.

"And as He drew near, seeing the city, He wept over it" (Luke 19:41). Yeshua lamented over the lost inhabitants of the city of Jerusalem. He saw their fate and grief overcame him. But the familiar passage "Yeshua wept" in John 11 does not use the word *klaio*. Yeshua does not grieve at the tomb of Lazarus because physical death is not worth grief. It is of no more consequence than sleep. Grief is reserved for those who are without God.

The daughters of Jerusalem wept because they saw the inevitable procession toward crucifixion. They saw one of their own being lead to death, brutalized, tortured and helpless. They could not see beyond that wooden stake on the hill. They could not see the fulfillment of God's *glory* in the suffering of His Son. For this blindness, Yeshua *wept*!

Klaio is the word of *pathos* and of judgment. Like the mixture of blood and water, the sacrifice of the Son brought the grief of humble acknowledgement before the saving God and the wailing discovery of God's sword separating the self-sufficient from the insufficient. *Klaio* is the word for both sides of the coin. If we know what it means to stand behind Him and weep, we understand both the deep sorrow over our past and the deep relief over our fate. If we see only as far as the top of the hill, we will experience *klaio* when our eyes are opened to the eternal horizon hidden in the cross. And then it will be too late.

"Weep for yourselves and for your children," says Yeshua. Weep as I wept when I saw you from that hillside. Weep as I wept when I witnessed your rejection. Weep as I wept when the prophets were spurned, when the signs were ignored and the when the Son was trampled under foot. The heart of the Father is broken over you.

Too often our *pathos* gathers itself in the assurance that we are His children. Our confidence is built on the glory of the cross. And as we experience the tears of gratitude for undeserved grace, we lose track of the other side of *klaio*. We forget to weep over those who still do not see beyond the tomb. We forget to weep for those whose lives are entangled with the inevitable march toward death. In our relief, we forget Yeshua wept for every one of those who *would not* see the Way, the Truth and the Life.

The heart of a servant is never fulfilled in confidence of self-arrival. The heart of a servant is always open to the *pathos* of those who have not discovered God's reality in their lives. When Yeshua looked on these women, he saw their pain. That pain opened the way for understanding because it provided a tear in the fabric of life's illusion of safety. It was the pain of being held prisoners all our lives to the fear of death (Hebrews 2:15). By the end of that day in Jerusalem, death no longer was the victor. To be a servant of the King is to proclaim freedom to those who are still held in bondage. Daughters of Jerusalem, look beyond the cross!

When you stand before Yeshua, will you recall the times when you wept for the lost with Him?

INSIGHT

How can this be?

Tragedy often produces enlightenment. When we experience life's greatest heartaches, we are forced to reconsider our priorities and purposes. What we discover usually alters the way we live. This transcending experience seems to be the same regardless of culture or historical period. It is a truly human event. Because this experience reaches across the divides of time and place, we can learn from others who have walked through tragedy.

Yeshua teaches us a great deal about the experience of tragedy, no more so than in His interaction with one particular family He loved. When we read this story, we find our own emotions and expectations woven into the words of Mary and Martha. These women demonstrate the power of insight – and the difficulty of holding on to a revelation of the Spirit. Their experience two thousand years ago is as relevant as yesterday's news. This is a story worth hearing again and again.

The story of John 11:17-27

"Do you believe this?" John 11:26

In one of the greatest stories of John's gospel, we are given a glimpse of devotion, trust and love in a family. It takes tragedy to peel back the cultural protocol. It takes death to open the window for us to witness this tenderness, care and enlightenment. The first lesson for us is not found in the words but rather in the circumstances. It took the death of their brother to bring Mary and

Martha to a point where they could see beyond the tomb. They needed to grieve before they could gain insight into God's view of the grave. When we confront life's traumatic events, we share this geography with Mary and Martha. Suffering is the precursor to enlightenment. Should we expect that God would deal with us in more comfortable ways? Should we cry, "Unfair!" when life puts heavy burdens on our shoulders? Sorrow is the intended kiln of God's glory.

Lazarus is dead. Too late for Lazarus, but not too late for Martha to proclaim her lost hope. She runs to Yeshua as he approaches the house, saying, "If you were here, my brother would not have died." There is confident faith in this proclamation. "If you were here." "If" – the word of exquisite hindsight. Here in Greek the word is *ei*. It is not the only Greek word for "if." This word implies "possibility without the expression of uncertainty."[12] There is *no doubt* in Martha's mind that if Yeshua had just come on time, Lazarus would be alive.

Before we congratulate Martha for her complete trust in the healing powers of Yeshua, we must add a little history. Palestine was not a large country. News about Yeshua traveled from place to place, especially among those who were devoted to him. This is not the first time Yeshua met Martha. Since both Mary and Martha were counted as special followers of Yeshua, we can assume that they would be familiar with the other miracles Yeshua performed when he was not in Bethany. They would have known about the man lowered through the roof. They would have heard about the blind man on the road, the cripple at the pool of Siloam, the woman with a crooked spine. Would they not be familiar with the story of the widow of Nain or the daughter of Jarius? If Martha

---

[12] Zodhiates, Spiros, *The Complete Word Study Dictionary of the New Testament*, p. 505

knew that Yeshua already exercised power over death, why has her hope evaporated? The answer is all about timing.

First Century Jewish theology believed that the spirit hovered over the departed body for three days, after which no recovery was possible. So Yeshua delays four days. He waits long enough to be sure the superstition about death cannot play a role in God's glory. God's intervention cannot be revealed as long as human beings believe there is any hope within this world. By the time Yeshua arrives, everyone knows it is too late. This is the confidence and the desperation of Martha. She knows without doubt that Yeshua *could have done something*. But her faith is limited to her human horizon. So Martha can say, without any equivocation, "if only." "I believe, Lord, that you could have done something, even after death, if only you were here in time." Martha's vision is limited by the horizon of this world, even when that horizon is stretched beyond the grave. It is four days, not three. Now it's too late.

How much of our own lives are built around "if"? What is the stretched limit of our faith? When does God arrive too late? Are we not Marthas, standing in front of Yeshua, proclaiming our utter conviction that if he had just come into our tragic circumstances sooner, we would have been saved? "Yeshua, why did you wait? If you had just come a few hours earlier, things would have been right." How many times have our own prayers echoed timing limitations? "I waited, God. But You didn't come on time. Now it's too late." The horizon we see is bound by the curve of our existence.

Timing is a critical faith axis. We all believe that God *can* do miraculous things. But we are not so convinced that God *will* do them. It is a matter of timing. Yes, in the end, at the close of the age, long after we are all dead and gone, God will make everything right. But not yet. Our faith turns on the axis of timing. We believe – but not yet. Martha was no different.

And then Martha, the one who seemed too occupied with this world, the one who did not choose the "one important thing," utters a proclamation of faith that pushes aside human limitations.

"Even now I know that whatever You ask of God, God will give You." Martha stretches just a little beyond the three days in the grave. Even now, even after everyone else thinks it is too late, even when I can't imagine how, even now God will give. The Greek phrase is a little different. It reads, "But also now." The words are emphatic, direct, aggressive. Martha is straining beyond her own understanding. She is remembering the widow of Nain and the child in Jarius' house. "Yes, Lord, it's true that you have arrived when all my hope seems gone, *but even at this late hour*, if you ask, God will give."

Fall at His feet with Martha. "Lord, the circumstances of my life are so overwhelming. Things are beyond anyone's power to restore. It is too late.

My marriage is dead.
My career is finished.
My children are lost.
My hope is buried.
My life is ruined.

On every side, Lord, the tombs of life loom large. The time for healing is past. It has been *four* days."

And from the recesses of the heart comes the antiphonal chord – *but even now*. "Even now, Lord, if you ask for me, God will give."

We cannot place any more hope in ourselves, our understanding or our imagination. That time is past. We cannot even hope in our need. We can only beg that Yeshua will make a request *for us* because we have never stopped believing that *He* has God's ear.

When we reach the end of expectation, when we are no longer able to stretch our faith to cover the need, when our lives are so crushed that God has disappeared over the horizon, there is still this: what Yeshua asks, God will give.

Martha's faith was deep. But it was not anchored in her experience of Yeshua' actions. It was not found in the evidence of his power. Her faith was in *who he was*. He was the one that God answered. When everything shouted, "Too late!" Martha has only this to cling to – God would answer Him.

I know the ground where Martha stood. I know the place where it is all too late. It is the place where all I can say is, "Lord, please ask for me?"

INSIGHT (2)

"Do you believe this?" John 11:26

The literary technique is important. John uses the technique of shifting to the present tense in order to bring the action right before us. We are there, right now, witnessing the conversation.

"Yeshua *saying* (present tense) to her, "Your brother will rise again." "Rise again" is in the middle voice. English does not have a *middle* voice. We have active voice (the verb expresses the action of the subject) and passive voice (the verb expresses an action done to the subject). But Greek has a middle voice where the verb expresses an action that is of particular significance to the subject. "Your brother will himself rise again." Why use the middle voice? Because Yeshua is indicating that Lazarus will not rise on the Judgment Day as a liberated soul or a spiritual being. Martha is looking too far ahead. Lazarus himself, as he is now, will rise today.

Martha's horizon is still limited by her current theology. She answers (in the present tense), "Yes, Lord. I know he will rise again." Her religious view of the world included the great reckoning of God in the distant future. She had no doubt that someday justice would be done, that someday the grief of this life would be overcome and that someday she would see the one she loved again. But now, on this day, death held the keys that locked her brother in the grave. Martha sees this world and the next but she fails to see that they are connected today.

Martha concludes her religious conviction with these words: "in the resurrection on the last day." Resurrection in Greek is *anastasis* – to stand up. Death has laid him in the ground, but in the last day

God will make him stand again. For Martha, Life is now and Life is then. Between these two, death reigns supreme. Martha's view is broken in the middle. She might as well have said, "Yes, Lord, I know that you can take care of what I see now and I know that God will take care of the end, but in between, all is lost."

Yeshua paints a different picture. His picture is one continuous stream of divine ontological footing. John makes this point in the third verse of his gospel. "In Him was Life." The world is not made up of three parts – living, dying and rising again. That picture is backwards. The world is already dead. The transition is not from life to death but rather from death to life. Once we pass from this present death into life in Him, the event of physical dying makes no difference at all. Death is being lost. Dying is simply stepping out of the dead zone.

Yeshua answers, "I am the resurrection and the life." It is significant that Yeshua uses the expression *ego eimi* (I am). This is not the first time that these two words play a special role in John's gospel. They are the confirmation of divinity. The great I AM of Exodus is repeated on the lips of Yeshua. But Yeshua does not offer to do what Martha asks, even in her declaration of his special relation with the Father. Yeshua does not say, "I will give you your brother's resurrection." He says, "I AM the resurrection and the life." Yeshua is not going to be the implementing vehicle bringing about a miraculous act of God. Yeshua is no medium. He is Life itself. He is in himself the passage from death to life. There is no need to wait until the last day. *This is the last day.* Yeshua says that resurrection and life are not reserved for the end of the age. They are present in the judgment executed in this moment – the moment when you and I pass from death to life because we have moved from the world dead in sin into the world resurrected by Christ.

Martha's faith is the faith of future hope. It is the faith anchored in the desperate belief that life will make sense when everything is completed. She is the woman of "if only" and "but also." Yeshua is the Messiah of this very moment. His resurrection and His life do not depend on the "if only" hindsight of the past. They do not depend on the "but also" hope of the future. Where Yeshua is, resurrection reigns. Where Yeshua is, there is Life.

Once again we are replicas of Martha. We confront the tragedies of our world and claim the "but also" theology of the distant future. "Oh, God, I know that someday You will straighten all this out. I know that in the end, You will make things right." When we lift our eyes past the horizon of human vision, we skip over the continuity of His power and jump to conclusions we can absorb. Yeshua has to give us a different focus. We never had life in the first place. We were the walking dead. Our world is filled with the illusion that kept us captive to the grave. Yeshua tells us something radically different. "Until you come to me, you are not alive. Your life begins with me and it ends with me. Once you are in my hands, there is no past and future. There is only life in me now. Death is no more."

Are you caught in the hopeless past or the desperate future, waiting for the resurrection on the last day to settle the traumas you face? That is not "life in Him." Life in Him is the moment-by-moment calm dependence that is unshaken in transition, grounded in divine being. It is life given by I AM. Remember John's literary technique – it's all about the *present tense*. Yeshua is the resurrection and the life today.

INSIGHT (3)

"Do you believe this?" John 11:26

Sometimes life forces us to talk about death. It's not a subject we easily bring to mind. We pretend that death is on vacation. We deny the truth of our frail existence and our dependent temporality. But death shows up anyway. And when it invades our family or community, we discover something we already knew. Life is always on the edge.

This day, outside the home of Lazarus, Yeshua engages Martha in a conversation about death. Yeshua asks Martha to see her world not as the culmination of a tragic past or as the desperate hope for a distant future, but rather as a world in the presence of its true source of life. The real question about death, says Yeshua, is not timing. The real question about death is power.

Look closely at this conversation. Yeshua does not ask Martha if she believes that he is the resurrection and the life. *He simply states that he is*. Yeshua asks Martha if she *trusts* him because the question of death is settled not on the basis of a theology of the tomb but rather on the basis of trust in the man.

"He who believes in me," says Yeshua. But the English translation deceives us. The Greek reads, "the one *believing into* me." John uses the Greek word *pisteuo* 92 times in his gospel. Every one of those 92 occurrences is a verb. John is not interested in my "statement of faith." He is interested in my life actions. It's not about words. It's about deeds. The verb is coupled with the preposition *eis* (into). This is a word of transportation. I must go from one place *into* another if I am going to be the one *believing* him. My old world, the world that I thought was alive, filled with past traumas and troubles, must be left behind. I cannot be in Chicago and New York at the same time. Neither can my feet stay in Seattle while my head resides in Orlando. If I am *believing into* Yeshua, I must be transported into a new world – a world that is filled with resurrection life. The only condition necessary for this transportation experience is *trust in him*. But that does not mean that I sign my name to a collection of words. It means that my life gets moved. I'm not in Kansas anymore. I can't act, think, walk or talk like I am in Kansas. The sidewalks are different, the stores are different, the people are different. Everything about my life changes. There is no need for winter boots in Miami. Leave them behind in Kansas.

Most of us are baggage people. Go through any airport and take a look at the luggage lines. We love to take everything with us. Suitcase after suitcase, stuffed to overflowing. Amazingly, when we get where we're going, most of us just hang the stuff in the closet and never use it. But we still thought we needed to bring it along. When you travel with Yeshua, no baggage is allowed. He says, "I am the life. You don't need that old stuff anymore. Just leave it behind." We often try to take it anyway. Then God has to make sure it all gets lost in transit. Sometimes the losing process takes decades. But you can't arrive at the Kingdom terminal while you are carrying luggage. When you are transported *into* Christ, life begins again without baggage.

Death is the best reminder that baggage is useless. "You can't take it with you," we say. But we never realize that this is a statement about **life**, not about death. When you move from this dead world to the living world of the Savior, you can't take it with you. Yeshua made it quite clear when he said to Martha, "All ones living and believing into me shall not die." Be transported from here to there. Move from dying to living.

"Do you believe this?"

The question asks a good deal more than we might imagine. It is not a question confined to the realm of death. Yeshua uses the reality of death to confront us about life. We think that Yeshua is talking about life after dying. We think the sequence is living – dying – living again. But Yeshua does not see it that way. Yeshua sees it like this: we are dead until we find life in him. Dead – living. So we can go on being dead and pass from the walking dead to the not-walking dead, or we can pass from the walking dead to the living by moving from a world without Him into His world.

His question doesn't ask if we believe that he is the resurrection and the life. Our mixed up perspective on living confuses us. His question is, "Do you believe that there is only life in me?" "Do you believe that unless you are transported into me you are already dead?" "Are you living and believing into my new world?"

Lazarus, buried in the tomb, is the only person in this story who reflects the world as it really is. His grave shows us that the purpose of death is to point us to our own finite reality. Lazarus calls us to see the truth. We are dead now. Nothing that we can do will prevent the logical conclusion of this fact from exhibiting itself – except Yeshua. Lazarus in the tomb shows us how ridiculous we are. Go count your suitcases. All those things that you thought you needed for the trip with Yeshua. Then look at the ticket. Boarding pass only. When you get to the destination, everything changes. Nothing you had before is required. It is all dead. Yeshua stands before us saying, "Make the trip *into* life." No baggage allowed.

REMEMBERING

How could I forget?

God has designed life to provide endless opportunities to experience His handiwork. David told us that the heavens declare His glory. So do the events of our lives – if we have the eyes to see. But living through the experiences of His grace is not the same as remembering what we have learned along the way. Every one of us fights a constant battle against forgetfulness. We are vulnerable to the distractions of life, pushing us away from an awareness of His sovereign grace and abiding presence. What is true of us today was true of those who lived with Him. Forgetting is the "natural" thing to do.

Yeshua confronted one woman about her nearly instantaneous forgetfulness. In spite of the preceding dramatic lesson, this woman let ordinary circumstances and expectations of the natural life diminish her spiritual insight. Her reaction is just like ours. Maybe that's why we can identify so easily. Maybe that's also why we need to hear her story so clearly.

The story of John 11:38-44

"Remove the stone." John 11:39

Not even twenty minutes. Not even twenty minutes pass before Martha blurts out, "But Lord, by this time he will stink. It has been four days." Right back to square one. Just a few minutes ago Martha proclaimed, "Yes, I believe that you are the Messiah, the Son of God." Now her confidence vanishes in the face of rotting flesh. Do you ever wonder how Yeshua could be so patient with us?

"Lord, we can't open the tomb *now*! His body will stink. It's been four days. It's too long."

Didn't Yeshua just explain to her that timing has nothing to do with death? Didn't Yeshua just tell her that life only exists in him? Didn't he just explain that everyone believing into him would never die? Didn't she just say, "Yes" to all that? So what happened to Martha? Why is she back at the beginning, fixated on the number four?

We can find the answer by looking at our own lives. There is an incredible gap between knowing and doing in every life. We are no different than Martha. We might *say* that Yeshua is the Lord of life, that He is the only source of existence, that He has the power to change anything. But ten minutes after the prayer session, we look at our world and crumble into four-day failures.

Yes, Yeshua, I know that You are the real source of life, but this situation is just impossible. What can I do about this?

Yes, Yeshua, I said that You have the power over everything in the world, but how am *I* going to fix this problem?

Yes, Yeshua, I claimed that I wanted to be in your world, but look at how important all my past really is. I just can't let go of that, can I?

Remember the verb *pisteuo* (believe)? Action! Action! Action! Martha, remove the stone. If you believe, show it! Don't give me wonderful words unless they are going to result in faithful acts. This is the arena of believing. Act. Remove the stone.

How many times have we repeated Martha's reply? "But . . . it's been too long." We are creatures of excuses. Oh, God, I would have done what you asked, but . . . Oh, Lord, I wanted to do what you said, but . . . There is always some reason to hesitate. There is always a dead body somewhere, causing a stink. There is always something we would rather not confront. Better to let it stay buried than to smell the rotten mess.

"Move the stone, Martha," says Yeshua. "Didn't I say to you that if you believe you would see God's glory?" But Martha doesn't believe, does she? If she truly believed, she would not be focused on that terrible number four. Isn't Yeshua fabulous? He shows her God's glory in spite of her failure. He goes forward in spite of Martha's failure to understand. Yeshua knows that we creatures of excuse often need God's glory regardless of our blindness.

Do you act like Yeshua? When those who follow you just don't get it, when you take the time to explain and ten minutes later your explanation seems nothing more than wasted words, do you still shine? It's a good thing that Yeshua was the one standing before the tomb. I probably would have thrown up my hands and said, "What's the matter with you, Martha? Didn't I just go through all this? How can you be so dense?" Maybe I would have been a little less gruff (after all, there is social etiquette). "Martha, how can you expect me to do anything about this if you don't support me? Don't you know I need you to stand behind me? Your failure has ruined everything. We can't go forward now." It's so convenient to use someone else's failure as an excuse not to do what God sets before me. "Martha, you didn't believe. It's your fault that I can't do this."

Yeshua is uninterrupted by the failure of those around him. He answers to only One. "Father, I thank you that you hear me and that you always hear me." Yeshua intimately knows his place and his direction. He also knows his mission. "But because of this crowd standing around." Yeshua chooses action in spite of the lack of believing. Yeshua acts on God's behalf *because* they need to believe.

Human beings have such a preoccupation with the visible that we rarely see the obvious. God is patient. He shows Himself in order that our open eyes can really see.

We all know the rest of the story. The danger is to let the rest of the story distract us from the reason for the raising of Lazarus. The lesson is about "four." "Four" is the impossible number. It starts the story and it ends the story. At the beginning, Martha is overwhelmed by "four." In the middle, Martha asserts her belief that "four" is an inconsequential number. But in the end, "four" comes back. She crumbles before "four."

And Yeshua shows her that "four" is nothing more than the window of God's glory. God is never too late.

Have you faced your "four?" Is Yeshua saying, "Remove the stone" while you plead, "Lord, it has been four!" "Impossible" is the greatest of all excuses. But in God's world, "four" is just another day. In God's world, the solution to "four" is "three", the day, when everything became new.

Are you a fearful four or a trusting three?

EQUALITY

Why do you think I'm different?

In first century Israel, ethnic, social and religious separations ran deep. There were lists of people to avoid: those with unsavory professions, social outsiders, religious reprobates and, in particular, the unclean. Yeshua seems to have spent a great deal of time with many of these. Apparently our views of who counts are different than God's view. For centuries, just being a woman was enough to keep you on the outside. Women were prohibited from the halls of power, offices of influence and the pulpit. It is almost as if being female made you unclean. God blessed men, but He cursed women.

All of this misogynic theology must end. The inexcusable behavior of powerful and influential men who acted as though women were second-class citizens in God's Kingdom is perhaps the greatest sin of the Church. God has no gender bias. Yeshua's conversation with one woman calls into question all of our fabricated distinctions. If we listen to this conversation, we may find reason to set aside our prejudices and ask for His forgiveness for generations of sin.

The story of John 4:5-26

"I AM is speaking to you." John 4:26

The woman at the well. So much has been written about this story that its familiarity threatens to remove its shock quality. The longest recorded conversation with any woman is unusual because this woman is not one of God's chosen people. She is a Samaritan.

She is one of those on the wrong side of a centuries-old blood feud. Before we even look at the verbal exchange, we are struck with another anomaly. No one witnessed this conversation except Yeshua and the woman. Yet John records it with painstaking detail. How is this possible? Yet there it is – glorious, deep and compelling. Something very important is happening here.

The conversation itself breaks all kinds of barriers. No righteous Jew would ever talk to a Samaritan. Even more impossible was a conversation between a single Jewish man and an unaccompanied Samaritan woman. No Jewish man would ever have asked for water from a Samaritan since drinking from any vessel touched by a Samaritan would defile a Jew. No Jew would have endured the backhanded insults of this woman. No Jew would have invited the woman to ask anything from him. No Jew would have condescended to her excuses. No Jew would have suggested that proper worship reached beyond the Temple. And, no Jew (but Yeshua) would have ever said, "I AM".

The impossible conversation, from beginning to end. The conversation that breaks every cultural expectation, every gender gap, every social separation, every religious ritual, every historical heritage and every deliberate distraction.

It all begins with "how."

"How is it that you, a Jew, ask me, a Samaritan, for something to drink?"

The basis of this question is an assumed prejudice. Yeshua does not begin this conversation with any indication of separation. In fact, he does just the opposite. He steps right over the social, gender, ethnic and cultural boundaries and ask for a drink. He walks right down main street in Selma, Alabama, steps up to the "Negroes Only" drinking fountain, and puts his lips to the water. He walks across the road in Bosnia and greets an Islamic woman with a hug. He meets the gypsy family in Latvia and asks if they will share some wine to quench his thirst. He journeys to Johannesburg and sits down with an African woman under a shade tree. Yeshua knows nothing of identity and difference. He knows only lost and found. The lost come in all sizes, shapes, colors, classes and cultures. The found come in only one way – through Him.

Yeshua does not sing, "Red and Yellow, Black and White, they are precious in his sight." Crayola does not make a color called "Found." There is no bloodline that is Found Positive. And there is no religion that earns grace for Found points.

If you are among the followers of Yeshua, you have only one claim of your own. You were lost. You don't get a merit badge for being found. Being found has nothing to do with you. Someone else had to find you.

The depth of our sad state of being lost is often seen in the questions we put to God. This woman's question hides all sorts of "being-lost" characteristics. The first question reveals that she accepted the demarcation of gender, racial and cultural difference. She was the one with the prejudice. She framed the question in a way that portrayed her difference.

"How is it that you ask me?" Moses said the same thing to God. "God, why are You asking me? I'm not good enough. I'm not eloquent. I'm not a leader. I'm not capable." God put up with every one of Moses' prejudices because God chose Moses even if Moses did not choose God.

When Yeshua comes to you and asks for something as small as a drink, are you a woman governed by "how?" "Lord, how can you ask me this? Don't you see that I am just a woman, that I am not powerful, that I have no influence, that I have a family mess, that I don't believe enough, that I am not ready." The "how" list can get pretty long. Yeshua never pays any attention to the "how" list. It doesn't matter to him. The "how" list just opens our mouths to reveal our misguided attitudes, thoughts and feelings. Out of the mouth flows the real prejudices of our lives. That is the purpose of Yeshua's question. Let Him ask something so simple any child could accomplish it and we are instantly thrown into a whirlwind of whines. "Oh, Lord, not that."

There is an answer coming. It is not the answer this woman expected. It is not the answer she wanted to hear. It is simply *the answer*. But to get to the answer, we must get past the "how" list. Is Yeshua asking? Notice your reply. Do you start with the question, "How is it that you ask me?" Yeshua never asks for explanations. He asks only for obedience. We are the ones who are constantly asking, "How?" We have forgotten that explanations are completely unnecessary in order to fulfill a request. What do you suppose this story would have been if the woman had simply drawn water for Yeshua? "How is it that you" isn't necessary for Yeshua. It's necessary for us. It opens the window on our souls.

Are you standing at the well in your life and saying to Yeshua, "How can you ask this of me?"

EQUALITY (2)

"I AM is speaking to you." John 4:26

Yeshua grew up as a carpenter, but he knew how to fish. He knew that if you want to catch fish, you don't yank on the line too soon. You let the fish hook itself by biting just a little on the bait and then trying to squirm away. All that does is sink the hook deeper.

"Give me a drink." No hook looked more innocent. She took the bait immediately. "How is it that you?" she says. The question opens all her prejudices to the light. Right away we find that she is trapped by her culture, her gender, her reputation and what she considers her superiority. After all, she implies that Yeshua is a foolish traveler, coming to a well and not having anything to use for drawing water. Jews seem to be exactly what she thought – stupid bigots. Who could have guessed that Yeshua would use water as the bait on a hook?

The bait taken, Yeshua lets the hook sink a bit deeper. More water.

"If you knew about God's gift, you'd be asking me for a drink and I would give you living water." (John 4:10)

Do you know why it is possible to catch fish with bait? Because fish don't see reality. They see only what they desire – food. They do not realize that this food is a trap. The Samaritan woman was a fish on dry land. She saw only her desire to eliminate her problems.

John uses the Greek words *hudor zon* (living water). These words in ordinary usage convey the idea of running water. In the context of Yeshua's conversation, the woman grabs this meaning and imagines an artesian well with water flowing over the top that does not need to be drawn out of the depths. This idea has already been implied in John's story before the conversation begins. In verse 6, John says that Yeshua came to a well of Jacob, but the word he uses is *pege* (meaning "spring or fountain") rather than the word she uses (*phrear* - "a well dug in the earth"). The Samaritan woman fixes her thought on the solution to her problem. If she had an artesian well, she would not have to labor to get water. She wouldn't have to come to this well. Life would be easier.

While the woman is focused on her need, she fails to see the reality of her circumstances. She makes a mistake. She doesn't listen. Yeshua introduces the discussion of living water with a thought that passes right by her. But it is this thought that really matters.

"If you knew the gift of God, and who is talking to you . . ." (John 4:10).

"If you knew". When Yeshua begins to talk to this woman about the real meaning of life, he points out that her biggest problem is perception. She just doesn't understand God's gift. If she did, her life would be completely different. This woman hears what he says but she doesn't get it at all. She thinks she needs more information. But the word Yeshua uses tells us that what she needs she will never find by gathering facts. She needs a different kind of "knowing." So do we.

Greek has several verbs for "know." The one we are most familiar with is *ginosko*. *Ginosko* describes the kind of knowledge that we collect from experience. It is knowledge that we accumulate from trial and error. It is experiential knowing. That's what this woman wants. She wants Yeshua to show her *how* to get this living water. She asks for *information*.

But the translation of Yeshua's speech uses the verb *oida*. This is a different kind of knowing. *Oida* strictly means "to perceive with understanding." It is intuitive, full knowledge. The word is constantly used to describe Yeshua's knowledge of the Father. Yeshua is not suggesting that this woman needs more information. What she needs is to be fully aware. She is just a fish, transfixed by the tantalizing bait. Yeshua wants her to see reality the way God sees it. He wants her to see with heart, not just with her mind.

"If you *fully understood* the gift of God." The point is that she doesn't understand. And neither do we. We come to God with our needs. We think we need more information. We search for answers. We construct theological solutions. We write rules for living.

Do you think that the answers to your questions about life are going to be found by collecting more evidence? Are you searching for that one more bit of information that will make sense of things? Yeshua makes a startling announcement here. Life is not *discovered*. It is *revealed*. You can't go on a quest for answers, searching the universe and all its facts, and have any hope of reaching your goal. God *reveals* the truth as a gift to you. God is the active agent. You are the recipient. The only real question is this: are you listening?

When we finally perceive that life is revealed, not discovered, then what it is that God reveals to us? God reveals His gift. The word "gift" is *dorea*. This is the only place in the Gospels where the word is used like this, emphasizing the "free" *quality* of the gift rather than the *content* of the gift. This woman started talking to Yeshua by making the wrong assumptions. Her assumptions keep her from hearing his point. It's not about the water. It's the fact that it's *free*.

"If you fully understood the *freely given gift* of God." The last thing this woman fully understood was the word "free." She was not alone at the well in the middle of the day by accident. She was avoiding the other women of the village because she had a reputation to hide. She slept around. She was a gender outcast – not by the men who enjoyed the *gift* she offered, but by their wives and daughters and sisters. Her gift was very expensive. It cost her the only thing that mattered – who she was. When she met Yeshua at the well, she was laboring in the depths of her soul. She was living at the bottom of a deep well of shame. There's no life there.

When we meet Yeshua at the well, we are just as likely to miss the point. We want relief from the burdens of hiding. We rush toward the apparent solution without listening. Yeshua looks like he presents an easy way out. "Give me some of that living water. Then I won't have to come to the well." I won't have to face the consequences of hiding from others. I won't have to be humiliated. We want the water to make life *as it is* easier. Yeshua wants us to see that life *cannot remain as it is*. God's free gift changes who we are. It is not about providing an easier way to deal with our problems. It is about having a new source of nourishment – a source that affects all of the rest of who we are.

"If you really understood the gift," says Yeshua, "you would be asking me." Understanding is not about collecting information. It is about being in relationship with the One Who gives. The gift is free but it has no value unless it is taken. Cheryl Durham comments appropriately, "When we use the world to get what we want by ourselves, we lose the benefits of who are really are, and who really meets the need."[13]

---

[13] in private correspondence

The first step in this fishing trip is the question "How?" That question opens the door to our misdirection. God does not need to answer the "how" question, but we need to ask it. It gets the hook set. The second step in fishing is "know" – to perceive with understanding. So many times God presents a free gift that we just don't see. We are stuck on "how" and "where" and ""when" while God is pointing at "who." It's the fisherman who matters. He's the one who brings the gift.

Are you fully aware of the gift or are you running around looking for information? God's direction is not about more *ginosko*. It's about reflecting on that deep revelation from the living water within. God gives. That is the secret to life. When we fully perceive the nature of God's gift, life becomes joyful reception and continuous thanksgiving. We stop hunting when we start receiving.

EQUALITY (3)

"I AM is speaking to you." John 4:26

Do you want what Yeshua offers? Then go, get your past and bring it to him.

This woman wants that living water. Her motive is entirely personal. "Then I won't have to come to this well and work hard to get water." She still does not understand, but Yeshua is about to make it all too clear.

"Go, call your husband and come here." These are words she did not want to hear. If you want living water, you need to bring him your dying past. This is not the way she expected the conversation to go. The sudden change in direction catches her off guard. But to her credit, she tells at least some of the truth. "I don't have a husband." She wants that water. The hook is in. She is not willing to cut her losses and run. So she uses the half-truth evasion. "I don't need to drag up all that past stuff. It's enough to just deal with the present. Today I don't have a husband."

When we are caught off guard by ties that bind us to the past, we are quick to find escape routes. Nothing is worse than being reminded of those old behaviors we would just as soon forget. There is shame in the past. Better to leave it buried. But Yeshua will not let us throw our past down a well. He wants it brought up into the light because he knows that whatever stays secret has power. If you want to be free, you will have to give all the secrets to Him.

Yeshua calls her bluff. "Yes, that's right. You don't have a husband. You have had five husbands, but the man you are with now is not your husband." Her evasion will not work. The hook won't come loose. So she tries squirming in a different way. Flattery and red herrings.

First, the compliment. "Lord (very formal and respectful for a woman who just implied that Yeshua was a unprepared, stupid Jewish traveler), I *perceive* that you are a prophet." The word she uses is *theoro*. It means "to inspect closely, to look at attentively and with purpose." A good choice of verb, but in her case a condemning implication. You see (no pun intended), the fact is that she doesn't *perceive* at all. She is blind to the truth. She still hasn't understood Yeshua's first remark, "If you fully comprehended the free gift." So, she goes off on another tangent, throwing out a theory (*theoro*) without actually looking closely at the evidence. All she wants to do is divert the conversation from the subject of husbands. She calls Yeshua a prophet based on purely circumstantial evidence. Does the statement Yeshua makes regarding her six male partners really warrant the conclusion that he is a prophet? Hardly! Prophets spoke for God. They were quite a bit more than oracles of marital fidelity. Calling a man a prophet would make any Jewish male swell with pride. That is her purpose. Move away from the issue of her past. Get on to something safer – like religious doctrine. Something that has no real bearing on life as it is today.

Flattery. "Oh, now I see how great you are. Why, you're a prophet! You're special. And since you're so special, maybe you can answer this perplexing question about worship." (There, that will keep him going.)

Is it possible to *flatter* God? Flattery is the tactic of paying someone an undue compliment in order to gratify the ego. The act itself is unfounded, but it usually works because we are all so eager to hear how wonderful we are. It is deliberate delusion with a second agenda. Flattery is not about the other person at all. It is all about getting what we want *from* the other person. It might work with ego driven humans, but it doesn't work with God.

"Oh Lord, you're so magnificent. You're so wonderful. Why, you own everything. You have control of it all. You're the greatest, God. I worship you. And, by the way, I have this tiny little favor to ask." We aren't so transparent, but we often use the same technique. Just a tiny little something that I need done, God. It's really not much to You. Flattery must be somewhere on Dante's scale of attitudes from Hell. The servant of the Lord knows only one kind of praise – *from* the heart *for* the Father. Yeshua gave us a great parable about our "wonderful" efforts. When the slave comes before the master and hears the words, "Well done, my good and faithful servant," the response of humility is, "Master, I have only done what you asked. I don't deserve credit for anything more."

It is so hard to practice ego deflation. We are all so vulnerable to being told we are wonderful. Have you done a review of your flattery quotient lately? The scale has two sides – one that shows how susceptible you are to being flattered and one that shows how easily you use flattery to get what you want. Remember the slave and the master. The only real measure of worth comes from the Master's lips: "Well done faithful servant." The only measure of true response comes from the slave: "It is only what You expected." Anything else pushes us toward ego enhancement.

Her attempted flattery firmly in place, the woman at the well now employs diversion tactic number 2 – religious "Red Herrings." "Where should men worship?"

Amazingly, Yeshua actually addresses her attempted "Red Herring." All that flattery about being a prophet is only the setup to get Yeshua on to the topic of the proper place of worship. She knows that Jews and Samaritans have been arguing (without resolution) over this question for centuries. She doesn't want an answer. She wants a change in direction. If we were standing at the well and Yeshua told us something very personal and private about who we were, we might chose the same tactic.

"Oh, by the way Yeshua, I have been meaning to ask you about that predestination stuff. Do you think we really have free will or is God sovereign over everything?"

"Yeshua, if you don't mind, could you comment of eternal security?"

"You know, Lord, I am really confused about baptism. Some say it is immersion only, others say it is only a symbol. What do you think?"

Any topic will do as long as it isn't about our personal lives.

Yeshua cuts through centuries of debate. "True worshippers shall worship the Father in spirit and in truth." An incredible statement. But it isn't the knockout punch. Yeshua adds one more thing that throws the "Red Herring" overboard.

"For such people the Father seeks to be His worshippers." Did you get that? God *seeks* men and women. Not the other way around. We are not seeking God to worship Him. He is seeking us. The Greek verb is *zeteo*. Fervently hunting. God is on an eternal quest for those who will worship Him. He is the One searching the universe for true followers. What sort of people does God seek?

What does Yeshua mean when he says that the Father seeks *worshippers*? The word describes those who show reverence and obedience toward someone, who fall or kneel before authority in awe and devotion. There is no such thing as worship without commitment and obedience. True worship is not found in the music, the sermon, the offering, the hymns or the programs. True worship is life-changing submission. Wherever that occurs, God is worshipped.

The "Red Herring" swims away. Options for twists and turns are diminishing. The woman at the well begins to see. The murky water of her life is clearing.

She moves away from distraction and toward God. "I know that Messiah is coming."

Do you remember those two important verbs for "know?" Yeshua opened this conversation with the words, "if you knew." His statement used the verb *eido*, knowledge that comes from within, knowledge that is revealed deep in our souls, not collected from external evidence. Now Yeshua is about to reel in this fish. She declares, "I know." Her verb is the same – *eido*. She opens the door to revealed knowledge. She is no longer fighting to find some way around the external evidence. For the first time, she speaks from the heart.

"I *know from my heart* that Messiah comes." There is no definite article in this statement. She does not say that she knows *the* Messiah is coming. She says, "I know Messiah comes, the One called Christ." She uses "Messiah" as a name, not a title, as though she is saying, "I know Rachel comes." The Hebrew word *Mashiach* (Messiah) designates the Anointed One, the Supreme Deliverer who is God's chosen One, who fulfills all the promises of God through the centuries. The word *Christ* is the corresponding Greek translation of *Mashiach*. This statement implies that the woman is speaking hope from her heart. She is fully convinced that the Anointed One comes, literally, as a man who brings God's redemption. She has, at last, provided a platform for faith. From the depths of her heart, she makes room for God's triumphal entry.

And Yeshua fulfills her hope.

"I AM speaks to you." The thundering announcement of divinity. The being of God Himself given substance in physical form, standing before her at this ancient well. She is instantly transported to that moment in history when Moses stood before the burning bush and asked, "What is Your name?" She is undone. God has visited her.

When it comes to fishing, Yeshua is so incredibly patient. He waits, answering, enticing, directing until that moment of revelation when we step toward God with only the smallest inkling of faith. Then the God of power and majesty explodes into view. Our lives are dismantled in an instant. Suddenly we see. He has been there all along, fishing for us.

On this day, the woman from Sychar discovers that living water turns life upside down. She will never be the same. Her unraveling and renewal brings an entire village to Yeshua. One woman, one conversation, one moment – and everything changes. A woman's evasion becomes God's exaltation.

That well can be found in every life. It is the place where Yeshua confronts our deepest secrets and asks if we *know* that Messiah has come. It is the place where our past is purged, our present perfected and our future finalized. It is the place where we encounter the great I AM because I AM came looking for us.

SUBMISSION

Why should I serve you?

Yeshua encountered a woman rejected by others. She knew what it meant to be cast away, considered worthless by her community. When He found her, she was ready to die. She had given up on the life she knew. She was in a hopeless place. He rescued her, not in the way she expected, but in a way that restored who she was in His sight and gave her a purpose for living. This woman met the God who sees. It changed her life. She returned with the confidence that God determines our worth – and no one else.

Long before Yeshua was born in Bethlehem, He had a conversation with an outsider – an Egyptian slave who had run away from home. This is the first woman to speak with Yeshua. He asks her the two most important questions in life – the same two questions He asks every woman. It's time to ask those questions once again.

The story of Genesis 16:3-15

"where have you come from and where are you going?" Genesis 16:8

The last conversation we will consider between Yeshua and a woman is the first such conversation recorded in the Bible. It happened thousands of years before Bethlehem saw a baby in the manger. The Son of God, before He became Yeshua the man, visits a woman in affliction. Her name is Hagar and he is called the "Angel of the Lord."

The special phrase "Angel of the Lord" has received considerable theological attention. This title appears in the Old Testament fifty-eight times. It's not always clear if the Angel of the Lord is God since sometimes it looks as though the Angel of the Lord only speaks on God's behalf while at other times the Angel of the Lord is indistinguishable from God Himself. When the Angel of the Lord is a name for God, many scholars believe that these are appearances of Yeshua as God before he came to earth as a man. In this passage, the narrator makes it clear that Hagar has encountered God. At the conclusion of her conversation, the text says: "Then she called the name of the LORD who spoke with her, 'You are a God who sees.'" The English "LORD" is the translation of the Hebrew *YHWH* (Yahweh), the name of God Himself. Hagar's encounter with the Angel of the Lord is an encounter with Christ.

How did Hagar get into these circumstances and why did the pre-incarnate Yeshua visit her? Once again, this is a story about compassion.

Sarai and Abram (before God renamed them Sarah and Abraham) have waited years for the promised child, their son. As the story opens, Sarai makes a cataclysmic decision.

"Yahweh has prevented me from having a child. So, Abram, please have sex with my maid, Hagar, and make her pregnant so that I may have a child through her." Abram agrees to this plan and soon Hagar is pregnant. Then the trouble begins.

Anyone with half a brain might have guessed what would happen next. Just think about the family dynamics. First, Sarai decides that God is just a bit too slow in delivering His promise. She takes matters in her own hands. This action spells trouble even if her plans are accomplished. God does not need Sarai's help in order to bring about His purposes. Her decision to follow the rule, "God helps those who help themselves," results in a mess that is still with us today. If we are to draw any conclusion from this story it must be this: when human beings interfere with God's promises, the consequences are painful. Eve and Sarai are not the only ones who decided they knew better than God. Each of us repeats this fatal error at some time in life. Fortunately, the Angel of the Lord is compassionate.

The next person in this triangulation is Abram. He is anything but a bystander. Abram had God's *direct* promise that Sarai would be the mother of the child of inheritance. He knew better than to follow Sarai's suggestion. He is ultimately responsible for the resulting pregnancy, literally and spiritually. Like Adam, Abram is weak. Instead of standing up for his commitment to God, he took advantage of the offer. He allowed himself the pleasure of impregnating another woman at his wife's request. When faced with choice, he elected pleasure over principle.

Sarai's plans succeed. But the success is a failure. Isn't that always the case when our plans circumvent the approval of God? What we gain is nothing more than another loss. Sarai gains an unborn child, but the child is not of her body and the result is animosity and jealousy. Hagar's pregnancy publicly confirms Sarai's humiliation. Sarai can't have children but Abram can.

Hagar proudly exhibits her blessed condition. Abram knows he will soon be a father. And Sarai seethes. She goes to Abram with vengeance in her eyes. Her first words shift her responsibility.

"The violence done to me is your fault! I gave you my maidservant but now that she is pregnant, she ridicules me. It's all because of you, Abram. You should have known this would happen. You should have stopped me. It was your responsibility."

How often do we stand in Sarai's place and announce that our plans, now gone astray, are really someone else's fault? Rationalization makes victims out of criminals. We all know this story because it is ours. If things go as we expect, then we take the credit. But if they cause us grief, we pass the blame. Instead of seeking God's forgiveness for her deliberate interference, Sarai seeks revenge.

"May God decide between you and me," she says to her husband. In other words, Sarai invokes divine wrath on Abram. "God will decide who is right. You slept with her. You are the perpetrator of this terrible insult. It's all your fault!"

Have we not used God in the same manner? Convinced that there is no fault on our side, we drag God into the messes we create and use His name to back our claim.

The first lesson in this story is the lesson of submission. Two women play opposing roles. A man and an Angel stand in the middle. The first woman, Sarai, shows us the destructive power of self-sufficiency, disobedience and jealousy. There is no repentance, no remorse, no renewal. Without these acts of humility, there is only revenge.

I beg you not to ignore this picture of Sarai! When we step into God's shoes and attempt to direct the affairs of life, disaster must take us to our knees. We must end up confessing our desire to be gods and give the world back to Him. No one can be God's emissary with a Sarai-syndrome.

SUBMISSION (2)

"where have you come from and where are you going?" Genesis 16:8

Sarai will not submit. She thinks she knows where she is going.

Abram will not stand firm. He acts as though he doesn't care where he is going. The first man in the middle is as weak in response as he was in agreement. His moral character is marked by another failure.

"God will decide between you and me," says Sarai. In this game of marital poker, Abram folds. He actually holds the winning hand, but he is afraid to play it.

Abram knows that God has promised a child. God's promise does not require intercourse with Hagar. But once Abram takes advantage of that opportunity, his moral position is compromised. The slippery slope keeps him sliding.

"She's your maidservant. Do whatever you want with her." What incredible courage! Abram, the coward, is unwilling to proclaim God's purpose. He will go to battle with kings to save his nephew but he runs for cover from his wife. The man God chose to become the Father of the Faith fails as a role model of the suffering servant. He chooses pleasure and when that backfires, he washes his hands of the consequences. This man in the middle is anything but compassionate. His choices are about self-protection, not self-sacrifice. As a judge under God's reign, he fails.

Armed with the confidence that her husband will not interfere, Sarai abuses Hagar. The word in Hebrew is *anaw*. *Anaw* is primarily associated with the idea of affliction through oppression. The verbal form (*ana*) is used more than two hundred times to describe the action toward an enemy, pain inflicted by bondage, suffering through war and the distress of slavery. This word implies pain and suffering as the vehicle that leads to repentance. *Anaw* is intended to produce humility.

At last the story moves to Hagar. We know the rage of her antagonist. We observe the lack of protection from her husband, Abraham. We see her affliction. Hagar does what any of us would do. She runs away.

You work for an impossible boss. Your union representative is no help. You have only followed the directions of someone else, but now you are the one who is getting the blame. There are reprisals you do not deserve. You are in "Hagar hell." You decide to quit and move away.

Your family life is abusive. You want to do the right thing but your husband criticizes you at every turn. Your church won't intercede. Your in-laws don't believe you. You might as well be Hagar's sister. You pack your suitcase and drive – anywhere.

Hagar heads for the wilderness. Throughout the Bible, the wilderness is a special place of spiritual warfare. It is the place where we encounter God. It is the place of confrontation, commission and submission. Unless we journey to the wilderness, we are not likely to meet the God of compassion. But most of us prefer resort destinations. So God has to engineer our lives to push us toward the wilderness. That push usually comes in the form of *anaw*. The motivation to flee to the wilderness is the attempt to escape from affliction. It is God's method of travel planning.

Hagar runs. She has no particular destination. The wilderness is an inhospitable place. There is no room at the inn because there are no inns. But Hagar believes that anything is better than life with Sarai. Exhausted, alone, defeated and desperate, the wilderness drains her of everything she thought was important in life. Her past is no comfort at all. It is a memory of failed hopes. Her future looks no better.

And then she meets the other Man in the middle.

"Where have you come from and where are you going?" The Angel of the Lord asks an obvious question of anyone lost in the wilderness. What on earth would possess you to end up here? Where have you come from? Was it so bad that you traded it for this?

God knows exactly where we have come from. In fact, He uses our flight from the past to get us to the wilderness. With a little reflection, you will see this travel pattern in your own life. Asking the question "Where have you come from?" does not mean that God wants an answer. The question helps us *focus on our situation*. It shows us how our false quest for independence brings us to the wasteland.

God knows perfectly well where Hagar has come from. The problem is that Hagar does not know. She thinks she has come from abuse and abandonment. But the tents of Abram and Sarai are really the place of her pride and independence. Her previous dwelling is the place without God. It is the place of *anaw*, the place that begins the journey of submission.

"Where are you going?" By the time we get to the wilderness, we know only what we are leaving behind. We simply don't know where we are going. That is the nature of the wilderness. There are no road signs or mile markers. It is a dangerous place where we can easily become lost. But the Biblical tradition contains another important wilderness concept. The wilderness is also a place of *divine help*. The spiritual symbolism of the wilderness is a representation of the place between regret and grace. We are released from the bondage of the past, but this does not give us freedom. Separation from abuse carries us to purgatory. We have escaped from the past only to be lost without a future. We need directional help or we will die.

"Where are you going?" is the critical question of the wilderness experience. Buried in the wilderness motif is another vital element. The wilderness is the place of judgment.

Sarai came to Abram and demanded a judgment. "God will decide between you and me," she threatened. Abram's judgment is nothing more than passive concession. But the Angel of the Lord executes God's real judgment without hesitation. The wilderness is the place where God's judgment brings submission and life or rejection and death.

Hagar answers the question the only way she can. "I am fleeing from Sarai." Her identity is still tied to the past she wants to forget.

God fulfills the critical roles of the wilderness. Help and judgment. He meets Hagar, fleeing an old life by running into danger. He gives immediate help, direction and purpose. But it might not seem that way.

"Return to your mistress and submit." These are not words of comfort to Hagar. Without the next part of the conversation, these words offer nothing more than forced slavery. "Go back to being *anaw*." God's solution is not redirection to Disneyland. He doesn't offer Hagar a backup plan or a second route to freedom. He commissions her to turn toward Him *through* her affliction. He directs her to fulfill her role as an Egyptian servant and to do so as a symbol of His character in the midst of abuse.

And then He gives Hagar the motivation she needs to submit to this command.

"You will have a son. You will call him Ishmael because the Lord gives attention to your affliction. And he will be . . ." Hagar's son will live under God's protection. No matter what Sarai might do, Ishmael will be born and grow up. Hagar will be vindicated. Her child will survive. God promises.

Mothers can endure a great deal of suffering when they know that their children will be rescued. Hagar returns to Sarai. She meets God in the wilderness and the encounter alters the direction of her life. She goes back to face her abuser, not with stoic resignation but with hope. Her future has been assured. What Sarai sought to take from her, God has given back.

The story of Hagar's abuse does not end here. Sarai nurses her anger for this woman until one day she is able to send both mother and son back to the wilderness to die. The amazing part of this story is that Hagar is obedient to God. Hagar, the Egyptian, the slave, the one not chosen, the abused and humiliated. Hagar finds God while the Queen of the Faithful wanders in her own wilderness of disbelief and disobedience and distress.

Hagar shows us what wilderness faith means. Return, submit and *hope*. God sees your affliction. Hagar can submit because her hope comes from God. So can we. The visible horizon of our own wilderness is not the end of the picture. If God guarantees your hope, then obedience is always possible. Return and submit. God has seen your affliction.

Are we ready to follow the path of this Egyptian slave? Will we also say, "I am blessed because I have seen the Lord and I live?"

Yeshua and Women

The conversations Yeshua had with women paint pictures for each of us. These pictures are the full-color palette of the heart of our Lord. From these conversations we discover the importance of a deep theology of emotions. If we are to truly understand the heart of God, we will have to open ourselves to the passionate feelings that saturate these conversations. We must turn away from the sterile theology of doctrine and dogma and hear once again the pathos of human voices encountering the pains, struggles and victories of life as it is. There we will meet Him. There, where women speak of:

Expectation
Exclusion
Hopelessness
Rejection
Remorse
Loss
Thanklessness
Grief
Mission
Fulfillment
Connection
Worry
Blessing
Destiny
Insight
Remembering
Equality
Submission

Are you listening?

Made in the USA
Lexington, KY
17 April 2012